Crushed and Bleeding...
but

The
Anchor
Still
Holds

by
Darren
Shelton

ISBN: 9781790589104

D & L Publications

DEDICATION

I dedicate this book, first to my Lord and Savior who has never left my side, not for one moment. Even though I have not been able to go to church for quite a while or call on a pastor or elders of the church to pray for me, God has visited me in a closer way than at any time in my life. I would not be here without my Lord and His miracle hand keeping me alive.

I also dedicate this book to my precious parents, without whom I would not be here. I remember my Dad carrying me on his back up the steps when I was little, and teaching me so many things. My Mom would give her life for me. She refuses to leave my side when I am hospitalized. She has slept with her head on a trash can, or slept on the floor when necessary in the hospital, because she would not leave me whenever I had surgery. Even though she grows weary, her heart and prayers are constantly with me.

To David, my one and only brother, you have always been there for me, and I can never repay you for all that you have done. You have even physically picked me up when I have fallen, and held me up when I couldn't stand on my own. You have sacrificed, not only your family time, but your work time, by taking many days off work so that you could be at my bedside during my many surgeries and hospital stays, or to drive me to and from hospitals. You constantly encourage me, are always so willing to run errands for me, and the list goes on. As my older brother, you became my substitute father after Dad passed away, and I look up to you and admire you so very much.

You are my best friend, my rock, and I love you more than words can say.

For all the prayers, love, and support of family and friends, and even prayer

groups, many of whom I will never know, I thank you, and I am eternally grateful.

Darren Shelton

Foreword

My friend and prayer partner, Darren Shelton, is one of the strongest men I have ever known. At this current time in his life, the world may see him as physically weak, but not for long! I know his heart and his strong faith, and I believe, just as he does, that his healing is coming soon!

I was honored when Darren asked me to write this foreword, as I have been prodding him to write his testimony in the form of a book. Little did I even imagine how quickly and beautifully the Holy Spirit would flow through him once he began.

I didn't personally know Darren, until he was an adult, when I first heard him sing at the church we were both attending. I still remember the tumultuous applause and standing ovation when he concluded his beautiful song, "The Anchor Still Holds." It wasn't just that he had a beautiful voice, but, when Darren sang, we heard his soul. At the time, I hosted a Christian daily program in St.

Louis, and I asked him to be on with me and give his testimony, as well as sing. As I also hosted a Christian television program in Quincy, Illinois, I asked him to appear with me there, as well. I had no idea of his physical condition at the time and all that he had previously gone through medically. I just knew that wherever Darren gave his testimony, he blessed all who heard him, including me. I also knew that, one day, he would be writing this book, which will bless many others, as well.

Through the next few years, our families would become friends and prayer partners. We were very honored to be invited to his house to hear his father play the organ, while the rest of us had a glorious hymn-fest. When Darren's father went to be with the Lord a few years ago, though we were out of town, I just knew that we had to be there at the funeral. The Holy Spirit urged me that this was not only for Darren, but also for his mother, Louise, who has been his rock, second only to Jesus Himself! She has been with him, watched over him, and cared for him around the clock for most of his life. She still continues to do so.

Darren's story, dating back to problems since his birth, is intertwined in this book with his love of people, for his family, and his passion for automobiles. More than all of these is his deep unwavering faith and his love for his Savior, Jesus Christ. As you read this book, you may want to take time to look up medical terms. So much that he explains, I had never known. There are also corresponding scripture passages you may find beneficial to apply. You may want to take notes to share with others who need to hear this encouraging truth that Darren brings. Allow the Holy Spirit to touch your own heart, and, perhaps, pray for Darren and his mother, as the next chapter of their lives unfold. Pass this book on to someone who may be going through hard times, and who needs encouragement in their own struggles. Most will agree, as I have, that our own crosses to bear are relatively minor compared to what Darren and his family have been through.

If there is one thing Darren does not want, it is pity or sympathy. Darren is stronger in most ways than the majority of people I know, especially me. I have counted it an honor and a blessing to know Darren and his family through the years, and to recently visit with him, earlier this year, while he was in the hospital. As we have seen the precious bond he has with his mother, I cannot help but compare it to both the bond and the burden Jesus' mother, Mary, must have felt when she saw her own Son bleeding from the cross, viewing His excruciating pain, and being unable to do anything for Him. Because of Jesus, Darren and Louise will be the first to acknowledge that we all have a blessed hope. We grow stronger in our faith, as we hang tighter to one another and to our promise of healing by our Lord. This is why, in spite of the numerous trials and tribulations, along with Satan's attacks, Darren's book reminds us all, that those of us who have trusted Christ as our Savior can know, now and forever..."The Anchor Still Holds!"

Dr. Debra Peppers

"The author's depiction of a severe hemophiliac's life, with the disorder and its complications, is both accurate and very graphic. His ability to cope with all of the negatives is a tribute to his courage and faith. That faith was the bedrock of his ability to progress through his trials with the knowledge that 'God is good,' but even more, GOD IS."

~*John D. Bouhasin, M.D.*

I have known Darren Shelton for more than 40 years. I have personally seen his pain and suffering, but in the midst of his pain, I always see his joy and his trust and faith in God, in spite of the circumstances surrounding him. I have so often referred to Darren as a modern day Job. This man has been bedridden for over seven years, and has had surgeries too numerous to count. With all the trials he has been through and with all the pain he has endured, he has every reason to curse his life, but, like Job, his faith remains strong. This book, that is his story, tells of that never-ending faith in God that allows him to live through each day of pain and suffering with grace and dignity, and that also allows him to hang on to the promise of God that his body will one day be restored. His anchor holds!

~Kimberly D. Cheatwood

FOREWORD

"Someone is sitting under a shade tree today because someone planted a tree years ago."
- Warren Buffett

Someone today will be encouraged and enriched in their faith, because my cousin, Darren, has refused to sink into his pain...but has chosen to live with God's purpose and peace. He has pressed through enormous tests, and has a remarkable testimony.

As you read, you will question, "How could anyone work through the chaos and challenges of being a hemophiliac?" Truly, he has a message beyond all the misery through which he has persevered.

"Life is 10% what happens to you, and 90% how you react to it." - Charles Swindoll.

God has personally proven to me, "It's better to wrestle with your struggle than to wrestle with the regret that you quit."

That is the fight, tenacity, and testimony of Darren Shelton.

Danny Baggett
Pastor, Cousin

Table of Contents

Chapter 1   1
Hemophilia

Chapter 2   7
My Life as a Hemophiliac

Chapter 3   15
The Terrible Twos

Chapter 4   19
A Divine Miracle

Chapter 5
The Mischievous Threes   23

Chapter 6
All Hope Was Gone   29

Chapter 7
This is What My God Can Do   35

Chapter 8
Oh, At Such a Tender Age   37

Chapter 9
A Call to Commit   41

Chapter 10
A Near Death Experience   47

Chapter 11
Bitter Sweet   51

Chapter 12
Desperation   59

Chapter 13
Bilateral Knee Replacement   63

Chapter 14
Beginning of the Rainbow Covenant   67

Chapter 15
The Amazing Car Show   71

Chapter 16
No, Not Again   75

Chapter 17
The Unexpected   79

Chapter 18
Trusting in the Impossible   81

Chapter 19
Deanna's Wedding   87

Chapter 20
Complete Trust in God   93

Chapter 21
The Fast   97

Chapter 22
Visions and Dreams   99

Chapter 23
Earthquake Dream   105

Chapter 24
Angels Unaware   107

Chapter 25
Another Wedding   111

Chapter 26
The New Car   113

Chapter 27
The Farm   115

Chapter 28
The Car Accident   117

Chapter 29
Elbow Surgery   121

Chapter 30
Feeling the Death Angel   125

Chapter 31
The Loss of My Best Friend   127

Chapter 32
Honoring My Dad   133

Chapter 33
Honoring My Mom   137

Chapter 34
The Start of a Long Nightmare   139

Chapter 35
Nashville Surgery   141

Chapter 36
More Hospitals   151

Chapter 37
The Worst Day of My Life   155

Chapter 38
Yet Another Miracle   159

Chapter 39
Tests and More Tests   163

Chapter 40
Waiting in Expectation   167

Chapter 41
My Next Chapter   171

About the Author   175

CHAPTER 1

Hemophilia

Hemophilia is an ancient hemorrhagic disease that most people have not often heard of. If you were to ask the majority of the population if they knew about hemophilia, most of them would just give you a glazed look. However, if you were to ask if they have heard of the term "bleeder," then the reply would most likely be "yes."

Hemophilia itself is a royal disease that emanated from Queen Victoria who ruled the United Kingdom of Great Britain and Ireland from June 20, 1837, until her death on January 22, 1901. Queen Victoria is believed to be the mother of today's present disease that we now know as hemophilia.

Dr. John Conrad Otto, who authored "An Account of a Hemorrhagic Disposition in Certain Families," in the New York Medical Repository, in 1803, and also wrote another paper on the same subject in Cox's Medical Museum in 1805, is said to be the writer of the first paper that appeared on this subject. Dr. Otto describes a form of hemophilia going all the way back to 2000 years ago, when the woman described in the Bible, who suffered with the issue of blood for twelve years, was healed by Jesus Christ. It is believed that she had a form of the disease hemophilia, labeled "Von Willebrand Disease." However, there have been reports of women from the X chromosome having spontaneous mutations of full-blown hemophilia. It is extremely rare, but reported, nonetheless.

The form of hemophilia that mainly attacks women is Von Willebrand's disease. This is why the woman in the Bible bled for such a long period of time. She spent all that she had on doctors in search of cure, but she knew that, by her faith in God, if she could just make her way through the multitude and touch the hem of the garment that Jesus wore, she would be made whole. At her touch of His garment, Jesus felt the virtue go out of his body, and said to the disciples, "Who touched me?" The disciples answered Jesus saying, "Master, there is a multitude of people that are trying to touch you." Jesus replied, "I felt the virtue go out of my body, and the person who touched me was instantly made whole."

Primarily, women are carriers of hemophilia through the XX chromosome. Friedrich Hopff, a student of the University of Zurich, and his professors were credited in coining the term "haemorrhaphilia." The term was later shortened to the word "hemophilia." In 1926, Professor Nelson, a professor from Finland, discovered the form of hemophilia called Von Willebrand's disease. This discovery was published in a paper, and was described as a pseudo-hemophilia, a bleeding disorder determining women to be carriers, but dominant in men. It wasn't until 1957, when another professor, as well as Professor Nelson, named Von Willebrand's disease, and their colleagues at the University Hospital in Sweden determined that Von Willebrand's disease was caused by low levels of proteins or factor deficiency.

Queen Victoria's eldest son, Leopold, died at the age of 30 from a cerebral hemorrhage after a fall from his wheelchair. Queen Victoria's nine daughters, especially daughters, Alice and Beatrice, passed on the trait to several of their male children. Alice's daughter, Alex, married Tsar Nicholas of Russia, and the disease was then carried to the Tsar of Russia's male children. All of these problems were caused by trying to keep up the genetic codes of their families by often marrying first cousins, and, in some cases, even marrying their brothers and sisters.

In the early 1900s, there was no way to store blood. People with hemophilia who needed transfusions typically received fresh whole blood from their family members. The life expectancy of male hemophiliacs was an average of 13 years of age. In 1901, the United States Surgeon General catalog listed time-inhaled oxygen in an attempt to use the thyroid gland, or gelatin, as a treatment for hemophilia. All of these experimental treatments were unsuccessful.

By the 1930s, experimenting with diluted snake venom to use as a clotting agent was tried, but this treatment was unsuccessful, as well. All of the experimental treatments that were used in patients with hemophilia, of course, failed. It was already known, by 1926, that there were factors, or proteins, contained in the blood that make it clot normally, but no method of duplicating those factors or proteins had yet been discovered.

Physicians discovered that patients reported repeatedly using direct blood infusions, given promptly from their families' blood, in an attempt to stop bleeding in the joints and muscle bleeds, but this treatment also did not work due to the vast amounts of blood needed.

In 1937, Harvard physician, Arthur Aptech, published a paper describing anti-hemophilia factor, which was found in whole plasma, to decrease clotting factor time in patients with hemophilia. Again, the amount needed was so great that an unlimited supply, at best, was a failure. By the 1950s and the 1960s, hospitals began transfusing fresh frozen plasma in patients with hemophilia. However, each bag of plasma contained so little of the necessary clotting factor that huge volumes of plasma were needed to be administered in a vague attempt to stop the bleeding.

Many children experienced severe muscle and joint bleeds, which damaged the joints so severely that they were often left crippled for life. Many bleeds led to premature death. Intracranial hemorrhage was the primary cause of death for a hemophiliac.

In 1967, a new experimental form of clotting factor, called "cryoprecipitate," which was frozen whole clotting factor, was tried with success in lab animals. The Federal Drug Administration pushed for the fast track for approval.

CHAPTER 2

MY LIFE AS A HEMOPHILIAC

As you can see, being born in 1962, with this disease called hemophilia, was not the most optimal time to be born. I will go into much more detail later. This was the disease I was born with.

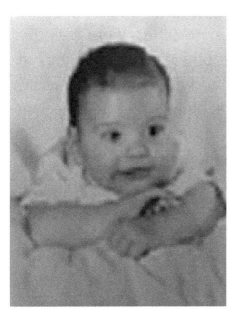

I had no other choice in my life, for it was already set in motion. It is amazing that I lived after birth at all, because one of the first things that they do for male children, after their birth, is to be circumcised.

Queen Victoria's male grandchildren died mainly due to circumcision and their inability to stop the hemorrhage. God had his hand on me at the very beginning to let me live through the circumcision. This might explain why, until the age of one, at the time I received the diagnosis of being a hemophiliac (a bleeder), I always had bruises all over my body.

At the age of two months, my Aunt Gladys noticed huge bruises on my back. It was thought, at that time, that I had rolled over on my pacifier, for there seemed to be no other explanation. At three months of age, my Mom and Dad wanted to take a trip to Maryland to see her grandmother, where Mom was born and raised. Of course, they did not have a crib for me, so they laid me on a pallet on the floor. All of a sudden, my hand turned black, and was three times its normal size. My cousins, as well as my brother, were called in to see if they had stepped on me. They, of course, were surprised, and absolutely denied the incident. No one could explain why my hand was swollen. A neighbor then brought a crib over for me to use, but the damage had already been done. No one ever knew why my hand was hemorrhaging. I was screaming in pain. I was rushed to the doctor, and he thought that I had possibly been bitten by a spider.

When I started to crawl, my knees would begin to turn black and hemorrhage. My Aunt Shirley, Mom's eldest sister, took me to her pediatrician, where she was told, "I think this child is a bleeder." His suggestion was that I should be tested to see if that was the case. In hemophiliacs, it is usually the firstborn, of the XY chromosome, coming from the mother, that is affected with hemophilia.

This should have affected my older brother, David, who is five years my elder. He weighed in at a hefty 8 lbs. 12 oz. He was a miracle himself, because the doctor came out, and remarked to my father, "Which one do you want me to save?" Mom was bleeding out, and had almost bled to death, having such a large baby. God intervened, and saved both my mother and David. However, my mother was told, "Don't ever have another child this large again." Mom and dad did not get any sleep for the first two years of David's life, because, although he had escaped hemophilia, he was allergic to almost everything. In those early years of his life, he would develop a 106 degree fever with every tooth that he cut, as well as every virus and flu bug that was going around. All the doctors could do at that time, was to tell Mom and Dad to put David in the bathtub, and give him an enema every 20 minutes in an attempt to try to bring down the fever. To complicate this issue, all of the fevers were only treatable with the medication called penicillin. As it turned out, he was highly allergic to penicillin, and it would have killed him.

Even though the doctors had told Mom and Dad not to have another child as large as David, four and a half years later, when it was time for me to be born, I came in at a bouncing 9 lbs. 1 oz.! Thank the good Lord, I came out seemingly normal and healthy, or so Mom and Dad thought at the time. David, now 61 years of age, has battled guilt, because he was not born with hemophilia. It is usually the firstborn, as I mentioned earlier, that is stricken with the disease. David does still have some allergy problems to grass, dog and cat hair, and various other allergies, but, otherwise, he is extremely healthy and always has been.

It was thought that Mom was the carrier of the disease hemophilia. However, it turned out that she, indeed, was not the carrier. This sometimes happens in hemophiliacs, and it is called spontaneous mutation. My mother also has six sisters, which normally would mean that one or more of them should have been a carrier, but none of them turned out to be carriers of hemophilia. None of my male cousins, going back four generations, have hemophilia, either, and are all perfectly healthy. In fact, we cannot find a single case of hemophilia in my family tree. Why was I the only one born with hemophilia in our family? Only God knows the answer to this question.

I personally feel that I have a great testimony to give, and I fully believe that I am going to be completely healed of this disease. I have faith to believe that my body will be restored from the damage that has been done to my joints. There is no doubt about it, God is going to get the glory out of what has happened with this disease, hemophilia, and its effect on me! I do not wish this disease on anyone, for the continuous bleeds and pain are unbearable. The only way that I can describe it is to liken it to kidney stones, but the pain is much greater. It is as if you are having an arm or leg amputated without anesthesia. What happens is that the small blood vessels break, and the bleeding goes into the joint, filling it with blood. My blood is not thick or thin - it is normal. In fact, my blood is O positive, but the proteins that are missing are clotting factor number eight, which causes the most severe form of hemophilia. There are a series of proteins in the blood called factors, listed one through twelve. I was born without the clotting factor number known as clotting factor eight. This means that eight through twelve were not activated in my body. It's like breaking a chain-link.

After my aunt's doctor made the comment that he thought that I may be a bleeder, we came back to St. Louis to go to a clinic so that I could be tested fully. The doctor ran a series of tests to see if it was possible that I was indeed a bleeder. They pricked my finger, they pricked my ear, and they ran a myriad of tests on clotting time to see what the results would be. On a normal child, the bleeding time would normally be somewhere in the neighborhood of 1 to 1-1/2 minutes. I bled for 13 minutes straight, showing the first sign that I may have hemophilia. Test after test was done, and all came back with a positive diagnosis for hemophilia. A final test was performed to confirm their findings. It was at that time that the doctor sat down with Mom and Dad, and gave them the devastating news. Their worst assumptions had come true. My dad was sitting in the chair in the doctor's office with his elbows on the desk, because he didn't want to miss a word. As the doctor explained the test results, he told my parents, "I hate to be the bearer of bad news, but your son is a hemophiliac." Mom and Dad had never heard that word, so he went on to explain. He told them that hemophilia is a bleeding disease that you are born with from the XY chromosome, and that it is carried from the mother and transmitted to the male, the XX chromosome. But, as I said earlier, when my mother was tested to be the carrier of hemophilia, the test came back negative, concluding that she should have never had a child that was a hemophiliac.

The doctor explained to Mom and Dad that they were going to have to pad my clothing with foam rubber, and find the thickest carpet to install in our home to reduce the chance of any injuries, resulting in bleeding into the joints. He further explained that I would most likely end up in a wheelchair, within a few short years, for the rest of my life. This was devastating news for Mom and Dad. It was as if they had been hit in the gut with a baseball bat. They talked on the way home of how they were going to have to deal with the hemophilia disease, since there was no treatment for it. Just learning how to best minimize the damage to my body was going to be a hard task. They prayed and asked God for wisdom, and begin to take it one day at a time. Every time that I would, for example, have an ankle bleed, Mom and Dad could only stick my feet into ice water in an attempt to take the swelling down. They still could not understand why I was chosen to be a hemophiliac, when none of my relatives had this disease, nor were carriers of it.

CHAPTER 3

THE TERRIBLE TWOS

This time period is usually called the terrible twos because most children are in their exploring age and even though this is the time that I should be quiet and subdued as stated before, if there was any way to climb to the moon I would have done so. I was rambunctious. I was curious. I should have been doing anything to keep from having a hemorrhage, especially in my ankles. I didn't have any crutches or any other way to get around. Dad had to carry me from place to place. I didn't have any other way to be mobile when I would have a bleed. We had never been told that there was such a thing as a hemophilia specialist, so we were in our own boat as it were.

This is also about the time that my childhood friends would come over to the house to see if I could play. I didn't want to be different so I would scoot on my bottom to the front porch of the house to play board games. I would color or do anything that I physically could, even though I was in horrific pain. During the times I didn't have a bleed, which were very few and far between, Mom and Dad would often say, "Where is Darren, he's too quiet." They knew that I had gotten into trouble, some way, somehow, and they were right.

In the spring of 1964, my Mom did not yet have her driver's license. We were getting ready to walk to the dry cleaners, which was about one block away. The telephone rang just as we were leaving the house. She took the call, and, while she was on phone, because it was such a beautiful day, I decided not to wait for her. I climbed into our 1958 Chevy, bouncing up and down in the front seat. I put my hands on the steering wheel and pulled the gear lever out of gear. I was having a blast! The car began to roll down the driveway towards the house. David thought that if he could run around and get into the car quickly, and throw the car into park, he could avert a catastrophe, but it was not to be. David was able to open the door and jump into the front seat, but not in enough time to throw it into park. I was screaming, "Yee ha," as I drove the car and hit the gas meter, tearing it off the house. Mom was still on the phone, and began screaming, "Oh my Lord, I just saw Darren go past the window." She quickly made another phone call to the gas company to get the gas shut off.

When we finally arrived at the dry cleaners, I told the lady at the counter the story about me crashing the car. Mom explained to her what happened, and the lady at the counter began to laugh uncontrollably at the story. As punishment, I lost my driving privileges!

It's usually about this same age that children begin to talk, saying words like "Mommy" and "Daddy," and one or two other words. Not to be outdone, I was saying complete sentences. There was a 1932 Ford, five window hot rod, with wide-open headers that went up the street. My first words were not "Mommy" and "Daddy," but they were, "Un, un, hot rod." My parents should have realized then that speed was in my blood, as well as hemophilia. I always wanted to go fast. Believe it or not, at the age of 56, that feeling has never gone away. I still like to drive fast. I love horse-power.

CHAPTER 4

A DIVINE MIRACLE

When I was two, Mom and Dad were looking for a new car. The old one had many miles, and we desperately needed to trade. I was running through the parking lot, and, of course, tripped over the parking curb, causing a frenulum tear. The "frenum" is the flesh that is in the upper part of your lip. Since there was no clotting factor in those days, there was no way to stop the bleeding. I bled for eleven days straight. Mom and Dad would put me in bed with them, and would take turns sitting up all night, pulling clots of blood the size of an egg out of my mouth to keep me from choking to death. Back then, dad was not only giving his time as the church pianist, he was also a Sunday school teacher. He regularly had visions and spiritual dreams. He was so close to God that Mom would remark how she admired his anointing. Dad made the statement that he thought if he would raise his hands, he would be transported like Philip in the Bible. As I said, I had bled for eleven days straight, and was so weak by that time that I had actually bled out. It hit dad especially hard, and he said to the Lord, "If you don't heal my son, I will hang my talent of playing the piano and organ on the willow tree and never play again." The church at that time was so spiritual, and had healing and deliverance services regularly.

Mom was very shy in those days, except when it came to her baby facing imminent death. She then became as bold as a lion. As they walked into the church that Sunday morning, she brought me into the service on a pillow, and she told the minister, "You are not having regular service this morning. My baby is dying, and if we don't touch God, he's going to die." Mom then placed me on the altar, and the entire church fell on their knees, and they looked upon me as if I was their baby. They began to pray in one mind and one accord. Mom took me home that morning, and brought me back to the evening service. She again laid me on the pillow, and laid me on the altar. It was at that time that the entire church began to see God move, as they began to pray in one accord. Dad said he felt as if his arms were ten feet long, as they stretched toward Heaven. He could feel the power of the Holy Spirit as he played.

A lady in the service stood up, and began to sing in the Spirit, in an unknown tongue, and she was singing in soprano. Shortly thereafter, a second lady stood and began to sing in the same unknown tongue in two-part harmony, with the same words and the same timing. Within seconds, a third lady on the other side of the church stood, and began to sing in the same unknown tongue in three-part harmony.

A dear friend that we know said she heard the angels from heaven come down, and join the church service that day. A thick blue haze began to fall over the congregation. When that blue haze in the church began to hover over where I was, lying on the pillow, the power of the Holy Spirit touched my body. The bleeding became a slow trickle, and then stopped instantly. That piece of flesh, called frenum, in the upper part of my lip, began to close up without any stitches. What the church witnessed that evening, was a divine miracle. After I was touched by the hand of God and the bleeding had stopped, I was still lying lifeless because of the volume of blood that I had lost. There was a chiropractor there that evening. He told Mom and Dad, "Mr. and Mrs. Shelton, I think that you can take him to the hospital now. They can give him blood transfusions for the amount of blood that he has lost." My parents took me to the hospital that night, where I received a transfusion to replenish the blood that I had lost.

Within three days, I was up running and jumping, as if nothing had ever happened. My God had touched me in my hour of need, and for that I give Him all the glory, all the praise, and all the honor. He, and He alone, is my provider for touching me that day.

CHAPTER 5

THE MISCHIEVOUS THREES

One year later, when I was three, it was Mom's birthday. She had decided to fry chicken for dinner. I didn't want to be cooped up in the house. It was a beautiful day with not a cloud in the sky. Mom was wanting me to stay close where she could keep an eye on me. Are you kidding me? It's not that I was a mischievous child. I didn't want to break things. I did know right from wrong, but I knew just enough to understand that I would be in trouble for causing problems at an early age. For example, I didn't go into the laundry room and open up the bottle of bleach and pour it the floor, or pour it on myself. It seemed that I knew right from wrong and danger, but Mom and Dad knew that I had to be careful, but I was always curious about everything.

I decided to go into my bedroom to see what fun I could find to do in there. I crawled up on my bed, and found that this bed had magical properties. If you bounced on this thing, you could fly higher and higher, and the higher you bounce, the higher you could fly, and the more fun you could have. I was having such a good time. All of a sudden, Mom heard a big loud crack in the bedroom. I had jumped almost all the way to the ceiling; when I came down, I hit my head on the headboard, splitting my head wide open. Mom grabbed me in her arms. She had no way to stop the hemorrhaging, and blood began to squirt everywhere. She started interceding in prayer like never before, pleading the name of Jesus to perform a miracle for her baby. As she continued to pray, the blood that was spewing out began to slow to a trickle, and then it stopped altogether. It was truly a miracle.

At that time, my dad and my uncle, Allen, came in from work. They grabbed me out of Mom's arms, and took me to the clinic. There they put fifteen stitches in my head to sew up the wound, and to keep it from getting infected. It wasn't but just a few days later, I crawled into the backseat of the car and started jumping up and down. Sure enough, I hit the back of my head where those fresh stitches were, and my head burst wide open again. Back to the clinic we went, where they had to re-stitch my head.

My dad was a master journeyman carpenter, and he began to build a brand-new, two-story colonial home. It was a masterpiece, like something that you would see on Pennsylvania Avenue. His talents were renowned. I begged every day to be in his shadow and follow him everywhere he went. Of course, this was not possible all the time, because he did not want me to get hurt. This is when, at the age of three, I would always ask Dad the word he hated to hear the most, which was "why." He would always say, "You're driving me crazy." He was always trying to find something for me to do to keep me occupied, yet not let me get harmed in any way.

I remember one time, when he took two 2 x 4 blocks and began to nail them together. I grabbed a hammer to have something to bang on. I was going to help build this house. He thought that would keep me occupied. But little Darren could find trouble where trouble didn't exist. I took the hammer in both hands, and hit the nail on the head once, twice, and, on the third time, I set the claw hammer into my forehead. God had to have had his angels watching over me that day, because it didn't even break the skin. It did, however, leave a scar that I wear to this day as a reminder.

The house was not yet completed, and Dad was working on the upper floor; all of a sudden, I was behind Dad, and began tumbling down the steps like a beach ball. Here we go again. God had his angels watching over me that day, as well, because I did not have a hemorrhage or a bleed. I was perfectly fine, thanks be to God.

It was an unbearably hot day in July in St. Louis, and the house was still not yet completed. We were living in our little house on Cady Street. Dad wanted to give Mom a special gift to celebrate their anniversary, which was on July 20th. The electricity had not yet been turned on in our new home. Dad ran an extension cord from our house to Allen's house, which backed up to ours. There was no carpet on the floor, just PFI plywood, but, nevertheless, he wanted to surprise Mom by moving the family into our new home.

As a special design, Dad had taken the master bedroom, and built the bed upon a platform. Dad had built two steps up to the bed. He told Mom, that if she got up in the middle of the night, to make sure she remembered those two steps so she didn't fall. In the middle of that first night, Dad was the one who got up to use the restroom, and He was the one who fell flat on his face. David and I were both awakened out of a dead sleep to laughter. We heard the loud crash, and knew something had definitely gone wrong. We went into the bedroom, and found dad lying on the floor laughing hysterically. I am so grateful for childhood memories, and times that I was able to laugh, in spite of all the physical pain in my life.

Bleeding episodes went on weekly, and sometimes daily, mostly due to the fact that I was a three-year-old energetic child. Bleeding in my ankles left me with the inability to stand or to walk. The constant hemorrhaging in my ankles caused me, at five years of age, to have arthritis so severe that I had trouble even entering and exiting a vehicle. I had to stand on the floorboard for as long as ten minutes before I could walk, and before I could sit down in the seat. I had to stand, holding the door of the car, until I could sit down. I had the ankles of a 100-year-old man. This made my life so difficult.

CHAPTER 6

ALL HOPE WAS GONE

At the age of five, I needed to have a tooth extracted. I was taken to a St. Louis Jewish hospital, where they ran a series of tests for one week. What is just a simple trip to a dentist for a tooth extraction for a normal child, was a major issue for me. They had no way to stop bleeding, or to control it in any way. The doctors were trying to figure out a way to extract the tooth, and control the bleeding at the same time. They knew that even if they would give me whole blood transfusions, it would not be enough blood to stop the hemorrhage.

After one week of testing, the doctors finally came up with a plan to pull the tooth. They planned to make an impression to slip into the vacant hole, in an attempt to make a plug to stop the bleeding. In order to make the impression, it required putting a gelatinous material into my mouth. I would also need to keep it in my mouth, and keep my mouth closed for twenty minutes, while the gelatinous material set.

The problem with the attempt to make the impression, was that the amount of the gelatinous material used was mistakenly the amount that would be used for a full grown man, not a five-year-old child. In other words, it was too large for my mouth. I immediately began to gag and to heave. As I continued to gag, Dad said to the doctor, "Get that gel out of my child's mouth!" The doctor said, "We can't stop now...we have to leave it in for a full 20 minutes."

Little did anyone know what was about to happen. After this process was done, I was sent back to my room, and Dad took Mom home to rest for the night. They had both been there for the entire week during all these testing periods. Dad came back to the hospital that night, after being there for seven days, and was going to stay until I fell asleep. He would then go home, and get some rest before my surgery the next day.

I remember that the television was on, and, in those days, they only had black and white televisions that required rabbit ears. It was the old fashioned kind that was run by quarters on the back of the television. A quarter would give you one hour of television. Dad was in the chair, sitting next to me, and the television was on, as I drifted off to sleep.

In the middle of the night, I woke up suddenly, and called for the nurse. "Where is my daddy?" I realized that Dad was gone, and the television was off. I had a strange feeling that something was wrong. The nurse told me that Dad had gone home to get some rest, and that Mom and Dad would be back first thing in the morning. It was at this time that I actually felt the spirit of death, for, little did anyone know, all of the heaving and gagging earlier that day from that gelatinous material had ruptured my spleen.

I was bleeding out and nobody knew it. By the time Mom and Dad arrived back at the hospital, I had fallen into a coma and my stomach was extremely distended. I was dying, and dying quickly. I was bleeding out. The doctors had examined me, but could not figure out what was going wrong. They said they needed to transfer me to St Louis Children's Hospital.

I vaguely remember getting into the ambulance, but I do remember that Mom was with me in the back. I was drifting in and out of consciousness, and I remember being put into an oxygen tent.

During that time, Dad went to see two ladies who he felt were very close to God, and in whom he felt confidence in their prayers. The first lady said, "I'm sorry, Jewell, I can't help you. I just lost my daughter, and I have no comfort to give you."

The second lady went on to say, "I'm sorry, but the Lord giveth and the Lord taketh," and had no encouraging words to give Dad. On the way back to the hospital, God gave Dad this word from the Holy Spirit, "Many among you are sick and weak, because you have not discerned God's body." Dad took that as confirmation that I was going to be alright by the authority of God's word.

Even though I was facing death immediately, God gave Dad the victory, and he knew that I would recover. Mom, however, had not yet received peace at that time. God gave Dad the assurance that, despite the circumstances, I would live and not die. By the time Dad got back to the hospital, all of my relatives were called from Alabama, Florida, Tennessee, southern Missouri, and from all over the United States. My Uncle Ferrell had called all of my relatives, and said, "Darren will be gone by the time you get here. Please come for Louise and Jewell's sake to comfort them."

Mom told Dad that life would not be the same without Darren. We were a family, with our memories, our adventures, and our heartaches, as well. I had been singing in the church with my brother, David, since the age of three years old. I sang tenor harmony, and we couldn't let our little singing group be broken up, let alone our little family.

The surgeon came in for a short consultation, knowing that she had little time to talk. She briefly explained to Mom and Dad that she was going to run a dye test on me. When the results came back, she said, "What we feared has happened. His spleen has ruptured, and he will be gone in five minutes if I don't get him into surgery immediately." They let Mom and Dad walk with the crib into the operating room. They knew that if I became upset or frustrated, that it could be enough to put me over the edge. I would be dead before I even got into the operating room for surgery. Before surgery, however, Dad said to Mom, "Honey, let's lay our hands on Darren and rebuke death," and that is exactly what they did.

They rebuked the spirit of death, as the doctors closed the operating room doors. I was rushed down the corridor into surgery. Mom and Dad said it seemed like an eternity waiting for an update. It wasn't long before the gastroenteritis surgeon who was on the case sent word down to tell the Shelton's that they had taken out the ruptured spleen. He also said to give Mom and Dad this word, "Believe it or not, this child has another functioning spleen laying right on top of the ruptured one." It was perfect in size, shape, and function!

I don't know if God created an extra spleen right then and there, or if God gave it to me when I was born. Regardless, God knows all things. He knew that, one day, I would be in this hospital, having my ruptured spleen removed, so He gave me another fully-functioning spleen. This spleen was not a dead piece of flesh. It was not a freak spleen, but a truly identical, fully-functioning organ.

This is as rare as having three kidneys, two hearts, or two livers. It was truly a miracle. They took out the ruptured spleen, and found that the second spleen begin to function normally. Within six days, I was doing wheelies up and down the corridor of the hospital in my wheelchair.

I had a team of doctors that came from other hospitals to see the miracle child. I praise God for there is nothing, absolutely nothing, that God cannot and will not do. He met me in my hour of need, and he healed me when I needed healing. He showed up right on time, when all looked hopeless. I give Him all the glory, praise, and honor!

CHAPTER 7

THIS IS WHAT MY GOD CAN DO

It wasn't long after surgery that I started kindergarten. Mom had taken a job, because finances were tight, and, yes, Mom had gotten her driver's license by that time. However, she didn't crash into the house like I did. I do remember that the teachers kept a very close eye on me. They did not want anything to happen to me, after Mom and Dad told them my life story up to that point. The teachers were worried that the other children may accidentally harm me. I was dropped off at the home of my best friend, Barry Yancey. We waited for the bus to go to North County School, where I started kindergarten. In first grade, the circumstances were basically the same. I missed so many days of school because of bleeds, but God gave me a brilliant mind, and it allowed me to catch up very quickly for the days that I had missed.

It was also about that time that I needed to see the dentist. Due to my hemophilia, most dentists were afraid to treat me because of the risk of bleeding. We finally found a dentist that was willing to take my case, but he refused to give me Novocain. He thought that it would cause me to start to bleed. I had to endure the pain of dental work without Novocain until I was 19 years old. There was no other choice, as he was the only dentist who agreed to treat me.

That dentist, however, gave me the name of the best hemophilia specialist, Dr. John Bouhasin, and for that I am eternally grateful. Dr. John Bouhasin was the most gifted doctor, and I would see him at the hemophiliac clinic, as well as at his office, until the age of 19.

CHAPTER 8

OH, AT SUCH A TENDER AGE

As I have said before, my ankles were so bad with arthritis, from the age of five until I was seven years of age, due to the many hemorrhages. I could not ride in the car without stepping onto the floorboard for about ten minutes before I could sit down in the seat, and had to do the same before I got out of a car. I had the ankles of a 100-year-old man.

Then a miraculous thing happened. We had a revival at Full Gospel Church with an evangelist by the name of Ronald Dougal. He was a very spiritual man who was used by God in the gift of healing. At the end of a service, he asked if anyone needed healing in their body. I knew I needed to get prayer for my ankles, but at the age of seven, I was timid. I went up to the front of the church anyway. Evangelist Dougal took a metal folding chair, and put it between the pews of the church and told me to sit down in the chair. I remember it so vividly. He put his hands on my ankles, and I felt the power of God and a strong heat go through them. I remember getting up out of that chair, and feeling no pain whatsoever. As I stood up, I remember walking back to my seat feeling the power of God all over my legs. More importantly, I remember for the first time in over two years, opening the door of the car, and jumping into the front seat without having to stand either outside on the gravel parking lot, or the floorboard, to get into the back seat. I remember that feeling, to this day, of the time my ankles were healed.

I have not had any arthritis in my ankles for over fifty years. God completely healed me of arthritis in my ankles. What I couldn't understand is why God chose not to completely heal my body that day. I started to have bleeds in my knees, my hips, and my left elbow, as well as in my right shoulder, but my ankles remained completely healed.

I feel that God was showing me, that though my complete healing may be drawn out, it was on its way. God sees the future, as well as the past and the present, so I know that my complete healing has been promised to me.

I don't want to leave out the best part of the revival. The following night after my ankles were healed, at the end of the service, the pastor asked if there was anyone that would like to ask Jesus to come into their heart. I am not sure how much sinning a seven-year-old could do. I had never said a bad word or done anything truly wrong, but I felt an uncontrollable pull to go down to the altar. I noticed that no one else went up to the altar to pray, but I did not care. I knelt down at the altar, and asked Jesus to come into my heart, and I asked His forgiveness for all of my sins. I felt the Holy Spirit, as He came into my heart, and I begin to weep uncontrollably. I must have been at the altar for more than an hour. I could not stop the tears from flowing. I knew that at the end of that hour, I felt different inside. I felt happy. I felt joy, more than I had ever felt in my life. I noticed that there was a puddle the size of a basketball of the tears that I had left behind on the altar. They were tears of joy.

I remember that I had a tape recorder that I had received for Christmas. At the time, a tape recorder was something new. I began to share my testimony by recording it. I did not know how else to express my joy, but I knew that I would explode if I didn't tell someone, so I put it on tape. My friends began to make fun of me, when I told them that I had asked Jesus to come into my heart. You see, I had to tell someone, anyone, how, even as a child, I could feel so differently after that prayer. How could I feel so much change with one act of prayer? That prayer forever changed my life. From that day forward, I have walked with God and I know that Jesus is in my heart.

Mom and Dad saw the change so much in me that for my birthday they bought me my first Bible. Although I didn't understand all of it, I began to read my Bible every day.

From the age of seven to twelve years old, every bleeding episode consisted of me going to the hospital to receive treatment. It meant having my knees drained, and three days of receiving a new form of a frozen clotting factor called Cryoprecipitate, a blood product. As I previously stated, this blood was not screened, and was taken from two thousand donors. This was such an ordeal that we held off as long as possible, knowing how devastating the hospital event would be. At times, my doctor would not be on duty, and there would be four doctors trying unsuccessfully to drain my knees.

I remember one episode lasting four hours, with doctors pushing and probing to hit the pocket. Finally, Dad told the doctors to stop. He told them it was enough. Mom ran to the phone to call Dr. Bouhasin, and asked if he would come to the hospital and drain the knee. As soon as he arrived, he was able to drain the knee on his first attempt. We thank God for our relationship with this doctor.

CHAPTER 9

A CALL TO COMMIT

It was in the year 1973 that God spoke to my Mom's heart to open the doors of our home for a prayer meeting. This was still the time my mom was shy and timid. She thought the Lord was asking her to start a women's prayer meeting. At that time, her best friend was going through an ugly divorce. I was always in need of prayer for horrific pain, with bleeding in my joints. Mom contacted her friend, and told her that she felt led to start a women's prayer meeting. Her friend came, and brought her sister, and a spiritual warrior that was so precious and anointed. Thus, they started the prayer meeting with four women. They met on a Monday night, and had a glorious meeting.

The little church where we attended had a wonderful minister and his wife visiting. They were very anointed. He also played the saxophone. Mom was always drawn to people that walked close to God. After the service, she went over to the visitor's wife, and asked her if she would come to the prayer meeting. She replied, "Yes," but later called and said, since she didn't drive, would it be okay for her husband to bring her? Mom thought then that maybe this was supposed to be more than a women's prayer meeting. She immediately called Dad at work, and said, "Honey, you must get off work early, and come and play the organ. I believe this minister is coming and bringing his saxophone." Of course, Dad immediately came home, and he began to play the organ as only he could. Between Dad's organ playing and the minister playing the saxophone, the music sounded like heaven on earth.

This began a Monday night prayer meeting that would last for ten years. It started off with four women, and grew to seventy-five people. When it started to grow, from room to room, Mom said to God, "Why did you call me? I am not a leader." The Lord said to her, "I did not call a dictator, I called someone who would be an obedient servant."

Mom would rush home from work every Monday night. She would line up the chairs, and move the furniture to get the rooms ready. Later, we outgrew the first floor, and Dad had to fix up the basement, because there was no more room upstairs. As the meeting began, Mom would read the scripture. She would have Dad play the organ, and we would begin to worship in song and praise. Each person would give their own testimony.

Miracles began to happen during those prayer meetings. Everyone that attended had learned about the prayer meeting by word of mouth. People brought others with them, and, each and every week, the prayer meeting grew. The minister, who was the first man to attend the prayer meeting, came regularly and brought other ministers. People would come from Illinois and the surrounding areas of St. Louis. There were so many miracles that people were afraid to miss.

I remember Mom saying to her friend, "Here's my door key; if we happen to be at the hospital on a Monday night, please use it." This was when God turned my mom into a warrior and not a passive person. We saw teenagers get saved, and turn their lives around, and many were delivered from drugs. A lady was once carried to the prayer meeting on a stretcher. She had malignant tumors in her stomach, and was unable to even walk. Her appearance was of someone who was nine months pregnant. A minister asked us to take a cup of water and all take a sip. This didn't sound like something that we would normally do, but we were being obedient and we all did as he asked. As we did, we watched the stomach of the lady, who was lying on the stretcher, go down like a deflated basketball.

In each meeting, lives were changed. We watched God do the impossible. We watched as the word was spread about the prayer meeting. Various church members brought their pastors to this meeting to see what was going on. The true miracle was that it was God, and not anyone in particular, who had control.

Each week, after the prayer meetings, and after most of the people had left, there were three or more that would remain to discuss the end times. We talked about how teachers were teaching children non-biblical values, and taking away our Christian fundamentals, the lack of morals, and even about Christians being punished for their faith and their Bibles being taken away in some countries. It is amazing to see what they were discussing, forty-five years ago, now coming to pass. We live in a time where there is no respect for parents, no respect for our flag or constitution. Evil is called good and good is called evil.

I can't fail to mention, on a non-spiritual note, that during those prayer meeting days, we also had delicious desserts that the precious church ladies would bring. It was a beautiful time of fellowship. What a wonderful taste of HEAVENLY MANNA we had during the meetings and delicious desserts afterwards.

The prayer meetings only ended due to some of the people moving out of state and changing jobs. To this day, years later, people are still talking about the unusual prayer meetings that started in 1973, and continued for ten years. The credit goes only to God for the miraculous things that transpired during those prayer times.

Even though my healing did not come during those prayer meeting years, I saw God perform what only He can do. We came away expecting the impossible and rejoicing with fellow believers, which made my heart joyful.

CHAPTER 10

A NEAR DEATH EXPERIENCE

When I was thirteen, I had another life-and-death event. I went to Dr. John Bouhasin to have my left knee drained of the excess blood that had accumulated. By the next morning, my knee had filled again with blood, so I went back to Dr. Bouhasin to have it drained again. It was highly unusual to have to have it drained twice in such a short amount of time. The procedure went something like this: he would stick an eighteen-gauge needle into the joint space, and drain approximately 60 cc of blood out of the knee joint. He would unscrew the needle from the syringe, if there was a little bit more blood in the joint space. At the time, I remember him saying these words, "Oh, my God, we have an open blood vessel." I was bleeding to death from my knee that he had drained. After emptying the syringe several times, totaling 800 cc, which is approximately thirty-two ounces, he said, "This is doing no good." He called the hospital, and Mom drove me to the hospital as fast as she could. We were unable to reach Dad at work.

In those days there were no cell phones. Mom never did drive in a crisis, but she had no alternative that day. Mom was numb, and I think God was driving us. In 1975, they at least had clotting factor called Cryoprecipitate. To complicate the issue, I also developed what they called an inhibitor, which is when your body rejects clotting factor. I was bleeding to death, with no way to stop the hemorrhage. They gave me massive doses of clotting factor all night long, not knowing that I had developed an inhibitor, which prevented the clotting factor from working. David had arrived at the hospital, and then drove over to where Dad was working to look for him. At this point, everyone had been notified of the situation, all my family had been called, and Dad, by now, had arrived.

I remember my family coming in one by one, and praying that I would not die, but live. In an attempt to stop the inhibitor, they gave me an anti-cancer drug called Cytoxan. The problem with the Cytoxan was that it was lethal to my body. I began to vomit profusely for seven days and nights at a time. For the next two years, until I was fifteen years old, every time that I had a bleed, I would have to go through the same procedure of clotting factor, then Cytoxan, then vomiting for seven days and nights. I may have two to three bleeds per month, so I was constantly in the hospital where I would have to go through this regimen over and over again.

The miracle of this is that, when I was fifteen, just two years after discovering the inhibitor, they decided to retest my blood for the presence of the inhibitor. It is highly unusual to test again, since, once you have an inhibitor, you have it for the rest of your life. To everyone's amazement, when they tested me again, they could not find any evidence of the inhibitor. I had been completely set free from this dangerous death sentence. No one in history has ever had an inhibitor, and then have it disappear. The only answer is that God healed me. From that day, at the age of fifteen, to this day, they have never been able to find any evidence of an inhibitor in my blood. If you are thinking they must have made a mistake the first time they did the test, the answer is no. The blood test was taken twice. In other words, I had it, and now I do not.

Having to live with an inhibitor would have meant that I would had to have taken up to ten times the amount of clotting factor that I now take for the rest of my life just to stop any small hemorrhage, making the inhibitor grow worse. I would have been living with a death sentence hanging over my head. At the age of fifteen, God showed up on the scene, and performed a miraculous miracle yet again. My God is faithful!

CHAPTER 11

BITTER SWEET

It was late in July when we decided to take a short trip to Maryland. We could never plan a trip before blackberry season. Dad always had such a big garden, and he would can the fruits and vegetables at the farm that he had grown. This year, we decided to go to Maryland. This is where Mom was born, and she wanted to visit her cousins. We learned that a famous evangelist that we had known for several years was now the pastor of a church in Washington, D.C. We decided to visit his church, while we were in the area. He was a man that was greatly used in the healing ministry. My cousin made the ninety-mile trek each week to attend this church, because they so enjoyed the anointed services that were held there.

Unbeknownst to me, they had told the minister that I sang at my church back in St. Louis. During the service, they called on me to sing. As I was singing, I noticed a beautiful blonde in the back of the church. She had heard that I was from St. Louis. At the end of the service, she quickly came up to me, and told me she was also a singer, and had, at one time, lived in St. Louis, too. I was thrilled at all the attention.

After leaving the service that night, I discussed the woman with my cousin. My cousin told me that she knew the woman's grandmother, and would call and get this woman's name and address. This began our correspondence courtship. After corresponding for a period of time, with long letters being exchanged between us, she decided to take a bus and visit me in St. Louis. Her dad worked for the Greyhound Bus company.

I was twenty-three-years-old, and had fallen madly in love with the girl of my dreams, or so I thought. She was from Virginia and I was in St. Louis. We lived a thousand miles apart. I would drive on the weekends all the way to Virginia, just to stay those few short days, then drive back to St. Louis in order to get back to work on time for Monday morning. They say that long distance relationships are difficult, but I didn't want to hear that. I thought that we could make it work. I was twenty-three, and she was eighteen. I drove to Virginia to look for a job, trying to do anything I could to make this relationship work. It wasn't long before I proposed, and we became engaged on February 2, 1985.

Instead of planning a wedding, we eloped. As you can imagine, Mom and Dad were in total shock after receiving my call to tell them of our elopement. They, of course, worried how we, as a young married couple, would deal with all of my health issues. They asked us to come back, and have another ceremony that they could be a part of. I contacted a florist, sent wedding invitations, asked my brother to be my best man, as well as asking my sister-in-law and niece to be in the wedding.

Dad did everything he could to make the day special. Dad cooked enough food, almost single handedly, for 400 guests. He walked Mom down the aisle, played the organ, and then helped serve the food that he had prepared. Dad was one of a kind.

On one visit, Mom sat my wife down and explained my illness to her, but, when you are in love, you oftentimes tune out those things you don't want to hear. She could not understand the sickness that I had to endure. Whenever I would take my clotting factor, she would leave the room. At that time, I did everything in my power to satisfy her, even walking miles to see fireworks when my legs were those of a 100-year-old man. I was pushing my body to do more than it could physically endure. I didn't want her to know the pain I was in, and I didn't even want to admit it to myself.

My wife loved to sing, and she would make arrangements with churches in local areas where we would go and sing together.

However, with her being so young, and being so far away from her family, she decided, after discussing it with her mother, to leave me after just two and half years of marriage. Needless to say, the divorce broke my heart, more than words can ever say. Mom and Dad had taken a short trip out of town, but, upon hearing the news of my marriage ending, and learning how upset I was, they turned around immediately and came home to be with me. My dad remarked to my mom that he had seen my body broken, but now my heart was broken, too.

It was at that time that Dad started having chest pains. It was also about the same time that I received devastating news. I will go into that later, but, first, let me say that time after time, at the midnight hour, God has proven Himself in my life.

Just four years later, my doctor advised me, after examining my medical records, that I had been exposed to tainted blood during the late

1970s, from the clotting factor taken from human blood donors. It takes up to two thousand donors to take the one ingredient that I needed, which is clotting factor number eight. The rest of the blood is used for whole plasma, sickle cell anemia, and various other diseases. The problem was that, during the AIDS epidemic, receiving blood from donors was a catch-22 situation. Little did I know, but I was being given clotting factor that had been donated from not only the gay population, but from drug addicts as well. They would sell their blood for $40. Every time that I would take the clotting factor that I needed to live, I was taking a 1 in 10,000 chance of contracting other diseases.

I also found out that I had been exposed to hepatitis B. When tested again, four years later, much to my doctor's amazement, I was hepatitis negative. This just doesn't happen, so you do the math.

In the late 1980s, we had taken a vacation to Florida. My doctor called me to find out if I had taken any of a certain batch of clotting factor. I informed him that I had taken half the shipment, which was approximately ten boxes. When I got back to St. Louis, I was asked to come in for blood work. Through this batch of clotting factor, I had been exposed to the AIDS virus, as well as hepatitis C. I was informed that everyone with

Hemophilia, who had taken this batch of clotting factor, had been exposed to both of these deadly diseases. Satan browbeat me saying that I had been given a triple death sentence.

Earlier that year, I found out that the cure for hemophilia in hemophiliacs was to have a liver transplant. Two individuals, who had been in a car accident, had to have liver transplants. When the liver transplant was completed, they were completely cured of hemophilia. Clotting factor is produced in the liver. When these two individuals had liver transplants, they were completely cured. Satan told me I would never qualify for a liver transplant, because I have been exposed to, not one, but three deadly diseases. All of this information was recorded in my medical records, but God had everything under control. Later, that same year, Dr. Bouhasin informed me, as he sat me down in the chair in his office, and said, "Darren, I have five patients in the bi-state area of St. Louis and Illinois that have been exposed to the AIDS virus from that batch of clotting factor."

I had told Dr. Bouhasin that I had taken probably twice the amount of factor as the other five, which greatly increased my risk of contracting these deadly diseases. He said, "No, Darren, you have taken at least ten times the amount of clotting factor that my other patients have taken." Three of the five patients that he was referring to had already died of AIDS, and the other two were only alive because of the medication keeping them alive. He told me that I had taken so much more clotting factor than those patients. Clotting factor is based on your weight, and, because I was overweight, I had taken more than anyone else. He then said these words that are forever embellished in my mind, "You are the only one of my patients that has remained untouched by the disease."

Again, Satan said to me... you have been given a triple death sentence. He tried his best to convince me that even if I was able to be approved for a liver transplant, that I would not qualify, because the doctors would consider it a no-go for a liver transport due to the fact that my medical records reflected exposure to these diseases. He lied to me, and said "You have been exposed to the AIDS virus, and it's in your medical records, as well as hepatitis B and C, and it will kill you." Satan is a liar, and is the father of lies. He will try to browbeat you at your weakest hour. I had just lost my wife, my marriage, and, even though I had been given such good news from Dr. Bouhasin, you can see that Satan was trying to place doubt in my life at my weakest hour.

I was told recently, by a disease specialist, that I was the 1 in 10,000 that he had read about in books. Even though I had been exposed to these diseases, I did not have them. It was called "non-progressive," meaning that, even though I had been exposed, none of the diseases progressed, which is indeed an answer to prayer. I am only free from these diseases due to God's protecting power. You see, He has a plan for my life!

CHAPTER 12

DESPERATION

Going back to November, 1993, I was looking for a Christmas present for my brother. I wanted to get him, and my sister-in-law, a clock for their home. My dad and I took a trip to a clock store about fifty miles away from our home. On the way there, I looked to my right, and saw all the new Cadillacs on display at a car dealership. I asked Dad if it would be ok if we stopped at the dealership on our way back from the clock store. He agreed, and so we stopped.

I had no way of knowing this, but the summer before there had been a three-sided sign located on the dealership property by where we had parked. The grass had grown over the spot where the post had been stuck in the ground the previous summer. As I was walking in back of the car to get a better look at the new models, my left leg went into that hole that was about two feet deep. I had been unable to see the hole, because it was covered with grass.

My left leg went into the hole, and my weight carried me forward. Even though it was cold, only about 35° outside, I began to break into a sweat, even though I was not even wearing a coat. Dad rushed to me, but was unable to pick me up. With his assistance, I was able to lean on the cars, and somewhat used them as crutches to get back to his truck. As I was making my way back to the truck, I heard something snap. I knew immediately that I had broken my leg. In reality, I had snapped my kneecap in half, but, of course, I didn't know that at the time. I immediately got on the car phone, called my mom, and said "Get the clotting factor ready, we are on our way home, and I have a severe hemorrhage." I had a bleed in both of my legs. Mom rushed, and prepared the clotting factor. Never had I endured such pain. I was unable to move, or to get to my bedroom upstairs. Not knowing what had happened, we called my primary doctor, who told us to go the emergency room to be x-rayed, but we were unable to move me to get there. In those days, no one with hemophilia just went to the emergency room, where most of the doctors were uneducated about the disease. Dad blew up an air mattress, and placed it in the family room floor. I slept there for the next two weeks, while taking clotting factor.

Unable to get up on my crutches, I scooted on my bottom. My sister-in-law, Peggy, took me to an orthopedic surgeon. She was able to get me into her jeep by backing up to the front door, and helping me to lie down in the back. She took me to Christian Northeast Hospital, where orthopedic surgeons took x-rays of both of my legs. They said "Darren, I don't see anything broken, but you have the legs of a 100-year-old man." This man was definitely not seeing what the problem was. In spite of what they said, I knew something was wrong.

CHAPTER 13

BILATERAL KNEE REPLACEMENT

During June of 1994, I continued to go to one orthopedic surgeon after the other, until my father finally took me to see an orthopedic surgeon that I had known since I was five years old. He did not x-ray my knee. He just stuck his thumb into my broken kneecap, and said to me, "Darren, I'm going to have to fix your broken kneecap. While I'm in there, I'm going to have to open your leg, and do a procedure called a complete knee replacement." I asked him, "Since you have to use so much clotting factor, and I have to go through the pain and rehabilitation anyway, can you do both knees at the same time?"

He said, "I normally don't do this, but if that is what you want, that is what I will do." I checked into St. Mary's Hospital in St. Louis, as I went through the rehabilitation process. Unfortunately, the physical therapist pushed too hard, and broke the staples that had been placed in my knee during surgery. On top of that, I got a staph infection in my knee, and this started a downward spiral. It took several months to get rid of the infection. This was a journey which I will never forget.

Mom and Dad had lost so much work because of all of my doctor's appointments and stays in the hospital, so they could not take any more days off work. They would prepare an ice chest for me with ice, water, and sandwiches, and then would have the neighbors check on me. They would call me every few minutes, and Mom and Dad would rotate their schedule to take care of me. Since I could not get up to my room, Dad rented a hospital bed and put it in the family room next to the bathroom. I especially recall one day when Mom tried to get me to the bathroom. When I went to get up off the commode, my knee jumped out of place. Mom said she would call the fire department or Dad to help me get up. I told her that if anyone tried to pick me up, they would injure me worse. I put my left elbow on the countertop in the bathroom and forced myself up. The pain was horrific.

There was an experience like this, it seemed, each day and so much anxiety for all of us. There were no cell phones at that time, and Mom had to make sure the house phone was near me always. I remember Dad saying several times that he would feel led to come back to the house and he would walk around praying and covering it with the blood of Jesus.

Dr. Wittgen showed Mom and Dad how to put my leg back in place whenever it would pop out until it healed. It was about four months before I began to walk again without assistance. At that time, I was walking better than I had in years, at the age of thirty-two.

I was very active in church, and was singing whenever I was asked. I felt great anointing as I sang. We had a wonderful church with special prayer warriors.

CHAPTER 14

BEGINNING OF THE RAINBOW COVENANT

I had been given dreadful news concerning my shoulder. My shoulder was completely destroyed from the effects of hemorrhaging for so many years. I had gone to see Dr. Wittgen about a total shoulder replacement. He was reluctant, at first, to do the surgery, only because he had not performed that many shoulder surgeries. However, my pain was so severe and I had such a limited range of motion, that he agreed to do the surgery.

I remember one Sunday morning at church, just before I was asked to sing, Mom got up and asked the pastor if she could speak. She shared with the congregation how she had interceded with God, telling Him that she could not bear the thought of seeing her son suffer again. She looked out the window during that time of intercession, and saw the most beautiful rainbow. She heard God speaking to her that this was her sign of a covenant with God, like the covenants given in the Bible. It was a covenant that God's hand would be on me from that point forward and with every surgery. God let her know that He would, in some way, shape, or form, remind her of that covenant.

In 1996, the surgeon and I had a long discussion about my upcoming surgery. I had even asked him if he had a videotape of what I could expect with the complete shoulder replacement procedure. He chuckled, as he said, "Do you really want to see what we're going to have to do?" I said, "Yes." He said, "Darren, first, I have to tell you that doing this shoulder replacement is not without risk. If the nerves were to be accidentally cut, you would lose the use of your right arm for the rest of your life." He said, "I'm not trying to scare you, but I feel obligated to tell you the risk that is involved." I let him know that I completely understood, but that I had no other option. Since I had no option, except to have the surgery, I wanted to know what he was going to have to do. The procedure required cutting into the joint, like cutting up a chicken and turning it inside out. This is where the risk was involved, because they could damage the axillary nerve. They would then need to drill down into the humerus bone, and place the prosthesis down into it, and then resurface the scapula and put in the other side of the prosthesis.

With all this news that I was given about my upcoming surgery and knowing the life threatening experience that I had gone through just two years prior, Mom told God she could not endure watching her son suffer like this. This is what she shared that Sunday morning, as she took the microphone and poured out her heart, asking the entire church and elders to pray for her son.

A member of the congregation had been on vacation when he saw the most beautiful rainbow. It was so breathtaking that he stopped his car, and took a photograph of it. When he came home, he loaded it into his computer, printed the rainbow photograph out, and mailed it to me as a get well card. He had no way of knowing that God had told Mom he would give her a rainbow as a covenant promise.

As I was preparing for surgery, I had such an unusual peace and calm in my spirit. It was then our pastor and the church prayer warriors entered the room. They took the surgeon's hands and prayed with him. The surgeon later came out, and said that he did not have to resurface the scapula. They only had to do half of the surgery, which was to put the prosthesis down into the humerus bone. Praise God! What an answer to prayer that was.

In 1996, Dr. Wittgen told me that the rehabilitation would take four to six months, but within six weeks, by the grace of God, I was fully and completely healed.

I began to share with the church congregation my testimony one morning, just before I sang. The anointing hit me, as I began to show how I could move my right arm.

For the next four years, I was living a pretty normal life with only a bleed from time to time. I was pretty active, driving my car, and going on vacations to Florida to visit my Aunt Shirley.

It has been 22 years since that shoulder surgery, and I have not had a single problem with my right shoulder. Praise God!

CHAPTER 15

THE AMAZING CAR SHOW

I must say, the years 2000 to 2003 were my most formidable years. I was very active in church. I was asked to sing every few weeks with regularity. I also had other interests, such as cars. As I said earlier, I have always liked to drive fast. I have always liked to have fast cars with lots of horsepower.

There was an upcoming car show in Dayton, Ohio. At that time, my brother had a 1994, 25th anniversary Trans Am that was white with a blue racing stripe. I had a 1994 Pontiac Formula that looked almost identical to his car. I would spend weeks on end preparing my car to enter contests.

I later purchased a Pontiac Formula and then I purchased a 1998 Trans Am Ram Air. I had a job working for a company called Mobile Com selling pagers, and was doing quite well financially when I ordered my 1998 Pontiac Trans Am Ram Air. The car had a six-speed manual transmission, which is something that I always wanted. It was the car of my dreams. I remember spending weeks on end working on it, even going as far as taking the wheels off the car, placing the car on jack stands in order to clean every inch of the car. I would wax the car over and over and do a process called claying, which gets every speck of dirt out of the paint. I would take Q-tips and spend a week cleaning every part of the interior. I would spend another week cleaning the engine, making it so clean that you could eat off the motor.

It was then time to attend the car show, where 500 vehicles from all over the United States, the United Kingdom, as well as Canada, would be judged. You could not be around the judges when they were judging your vehicle. In other words, they were judging the cars themselves, and that's exactly the way that I wanted it. I didn't want the judges to see that I was sick, and feel sorry for me to give me extra points because of that. Even though I probably had to work ten times harder than the other contestants, due to my health issues, I wanted my car judged on its merits and not on me.

I was so proud when I took second place overall in judging my car against five hundred others during the car show in 1998. I went back to the car show the next year, working twice as hard as before. Unlike others, I did not trailer my car, so when I drove the 390 miles after working for two weeks on my car to get it immaculate, I had to start all over again to get the dirt and road grime off my car before the judging. My brother, David, and his best friend Jerry, who lives in Dayton, Ohio, stopped by to give me a hand before the judging. In 1999, I again took second place. I was so proud that I had taken second place two years in a row.

At the church where I attended, I noticed as I was leaving one Sunday morning that there was an advertisement on the bulletin board announcing a car show that would be open to the general public. Everyone who knows me, knows of my love of cars, and they encouraged me to enter my car in the car show. The local car show consisted of about two hundred and fifty cars. I was undecided whether to enter or not, since I had just won my trophy one month earlier, I did not have very much time to prepare, but so many kept insisting that I enter and so I did. I took first place in Best of Show at that car show. As they called my name as first place winner, a man jokingly remarked, "I knew you would win, because I saw a fly try to land on your car and it committed suicide."

CHAPTER 16

NO, NOT AGAIN

It was shortly after 1999 that I began to have unbearable pain when I was walking, so I made an appointment to see Dr. Burge. It had only been six years since my bilateral surgery on my knees, and I was told that the procedure should last at least ten years. After the examination, Dr. Burge informed me that he had to perform yet another exploratory knee replacement. This time, he would be putting a larger stem in place that would go from my ankle to my hip. Dr. Burge was reluctant to do the surgery, because I had staph infection in both joints, however, in 2000, Dr. Burge performed the surgery.

It seemed the surgery went as well as expected. After leaving the hospital and being home for the weekend, the right leg continued to swell and hemorrhage so severely, we were at our wits end. Even after taking clotting factor and wrapping my leg with a cotton cast, nothing was taking the swelling down. We realized something was drastically wrong. The right leg was twice its normal size, and was turning black. I was in such agony and pain, the hemorrhage was so severe. Mom and I kept changing the dressings, until we had filled two trash cans full of blood. There was no way to contact our surgeon, knowing he would not understand the bleeding and no hematologist would understand the surgery. We hoped we could get through the night.

Exhausted, Mom was shaking so badly, and, after doing all she could, she went into her room and climbed into bed under the covers just to get warm. She cried out to God, "Dear Lord, there is no one to encourage me at this hour. It is 1 a.m., and I don't know what to do." She surely would not get any mail or get-well card as a sign from God, and there was no rainbow in the sky as it was still dark out. Immediately a song came to her that she had not heard in thirty to forty years. The song said, "God put a rainbow in the clouds." Again, God gave her another rainbow. How many ways can God show a rainbow? After each surgery, God would show Mom a rainbow in one way or another. This was God's covenant with her.

Later that morning, we went to the hospital, and Dr. Burge opened my knee and it began to spew like a geyser. He said he had to put his finger on the open blood vessel, and, afterward, tied it off. The bleeding would never have stopped on its own. I would surely have bled to death.

Things went fairly well from 2000 to 2003, though I still had periodic hemorrhages. I was able to control the bleeding with clotting factor, infusing myself, using a cotton cast to take the swelling down.

I was always active in my church. I also kept myself occupied, going to the farm with my dad, and helping him with his projects, like canning after putting in a huge garden. In other words, I was living a semi-normal life. I had a perfect family who loved God. We enjoyed singing and listening to the most wonderful organ music, played by my Dad. I stayed by my Dad's side, as he worked and built our home at the farm. I learned so much about his traits and his talents.

Around this time, I was introduced to a woman who had the most dynamic personality. Her name was Dr. Deborah Peppers. She was inducted into the Teacher's Hall of Fame for being the most inspiring teacher. Mom and I were overwhelmed by her, as we heard her speak. When she heard me sing, there was an immediate bond that drew our hearts together. She invited me to sing on her radio show, as well as her television program. It was such a wonderful experience. We were so thrilled and honored to meet her, and we remain true friends to this day.

CHAPTER 17

THE UNEXPECTED

In 2003, I began experiencing horrific pain in my left leg. I went to see Dr. Burge once again, and he suggested that he would have to do exploratory surgery. The surgery date was scheduled for December 29, 2003. Prior to surgery, Dr. Burge wrote his initials on my left leg. As I was wheeled down to surgery, Dr. Burge passed out. Another doctor rushed in, and told us that Dr. Burge had the flu. They were going to try to reschedule surgery for two weeks later. This was something that I did not want to hear, because I was in such agony. We then found out that Dr. Burge had pneumonia, and a nurse later told me that Dr. Burge had passed away. I have no way of confirming whether the nurse's statement about Dr. Burge was true, but I never saw him again. In all this, God had a different plan for me. If Dr. Burge had opened the leg, and saw how thin the bone was around the prosthesis, he would have amputated my leg that day. God stopped the surgery in its tracks at the midnight hour.

I then had to look for another orthopedic surgeon to perform the surgery. I went from doctor to doctor, hearing the same story every time...that an amputation was the only solution. In fact, one doctor informed me, after taking x-rays, that I only had one sixteenth of an inch of bone around the prosthesis. They all wanted to amputate. One doctor wanted to amputate the left leg, and, two weeks later, amputate the right. As we walked out in the waiting room, we saw nothing but amputees, but we knew that God had a different plan.

I then went to my primary doctor who suggested a doctor in New York, but he said, "Darren, you've been to the best. You might as well stay here." We went back to Barnes Hospital, and found an orthopedic surgeon that agreed to take on the case. In the meantime, my wonderful primary doctor had given me a product to build new bone. I had to wait six months for this product to work, but it, indeed, built new bone around the prosthesis.

CHAPTER 18

TRUSTING IN THE IMPOSSIBLE

Things began to spiral downhill in the year 2005. Prior to that year, I had felt like I was living a fairly normal life for the first time in my life. It was in 2005 that I noticed swelling in both of my knees. After Dr. Burge's passing, I went to Barnes Hospital and found another orthopedic surgeon who drained the fluid off both of my knees. He had the fluid sent off to pathology. He called me a few weeks later to discuss his findings, and told me that the fluid contained a form of infection called Staphylococcus. This was something that I did not want to hear. There was only a six-week period before my scheduled surgery. By the grace of God, I found a natural product called olive leaf extract that I began to take before surgery.

With only a short period of time before my surgery, I knew that my time was running out. As I have said before, the average time for a knee replacement is approximately ten years, but the knee replacements were only lasting me three years. You were only allowed, if you were lucky, a total of three knee replacements in a lifetime. This was due to the fact that they had to cut bone off each time, and there was no more room to cut. The week I went in for surgery, they had to do a process called "debridement" (the process of removing unhealthy tissue from the body). They had to open my left leg and wash out the staph infection that they thought was in the joint.

I remember the team coming in asking me "Who told you that you had staph?" I told them it was in the culture report, and they, in turn, told me that they could not find any evidence of staphylococcus. My only answer to them was that I had been taking a God-given product called olive leaf extract for six weeks.

Nevertheless, they did five debridements in five days, from Monday to Friday. When they got to Friday, my surgeon had left town, and said to me, "Darren, you will be in good hands, because I am going to leave you with my right hand man."

When I got back in my room after surgery, I noticed that I had a different hospital gown on than the one I had on before surgery, and that there was what they call a foley, or catheter, missing. Something had to have gone wrong. When they put me under anesthesia, I evidently urinated all over the gown. When they picked up my leg, they broke it. The last thing that my surgeon told me before surgery was that if the leg broke, he would have no alternative but to amputate my leg. Something had gone terribly wrong. I was screaming in pain, more pain than I could possibly bear. On a scale from one to ten, my pain was at a twenty.

No one could even touch the bed. I could not move, or the pain would be so intense that I would scream at the top of my lungs. They took me down to x-ray, and even the bumping of the bed being moved caused tremendous pain. Another issue was that I was as white as a ghost. My surgery was on Friday, and my surgeon would not return to the hospital until Monday. I was bleeding out internally...literally bleeding to death. They gave me two units of blood.

On Saturday morning, there was a very sweet nurse that came into my room. Now I am not being unkind, but she was a large woman. I knew if she got close to the bed she would bump it because of the small area, and I knew I would not be able to stand the pain if that happened. Instead of pain, this sweet nurse was used by God to bring me encouragement. That morning, at 6:04 a.m., that nurse said, "Darren, did you see the rainbow?" I said, "No, from where the bed is sitting, I can't see the rainbow." She scooted the bed down to the window, and there was not one rainbow, but two! It was a double rainbow that encompassed the entire hospital. In other words, you could see both ends of the rainbow, and the rainbow went over the top of the hospital. I explained to the nurse that the rainbow was the covenant from God to my mom and me. She got so happy she began to scream, "Thank you Jesus"...so loud that the other nurses thought something was wrong, and they all ran frantically into my room. This is such a beautiful memory for me.

I immediately called Mom and asked her if she had happened to see the rainbow that morning. She had not seen it, but I began to describe the rainbow to her, telling her that it was a double rainbow that encompassed the entire hospital. Mom began to rejoice. Again, God had reminded us of His covenant by showing us a rainbow.

The night before surgery, I prayed a prayer that I had never prayed before. I asked the Lord to send ministering angels to the doctors and surgeons, and give them ideas that they would not ordinarily have, and that in the event something went wrong, to give them new ideas. That is exactly what happened. As I was being put under with anesthesia, I was quickly awakened. The thing about anesthesia is that when you are under its effects, you are totally unconscious. However, I was screaming in pain while under the full effects of anesthesia, so my surgeon knew that something was desperately wrong. When you wake up from being put under, the first thing that happens is your hearing returns before you are able to see or talk. The surgeon whispered in my ear, "Darren, can you hear me?" I replied, "Yes." He said, "I have an idea. I'm going to try something that I've never tried." I replied, "What is it?" He told me that he was going to take the bone fragments, and weave them like a nail instead of amputating my leg. That was the answer to the prayer that I had prayed the night before.

He then went on and put in an anesthetic block in my leg that would remain there for a total of six months. I was not supposed to bear any weight, or even touch my toes to the floor. I was then put into a full cast for several months, until it was time to take the anesthetic block out and put in a new prosthesis. Even though I was still groggy from the effects of the anesthesia, I began to praise God for the answer to prayer for new ideas, and for my leg not being amputated.

The night before I went into the hospital I had been up all night. Mom came to my room that next morning at 4:00 a.m. I had spent all night praying, until I felt the whites of my eyes were scalded. Mom asked if I had been up all night. I told her that I had, and that I had opened up the word, not randomly, because that is not something that I do, but that my Bible had fallen open to Proverbs 3:26. That verse says, "For I the Lord shall be thy confidence and I shall keep thy foot from being taken." That verse was the answer to my prayer. After one week in the hospital, I was finally released.

CHAPTER 19

DEANNA'S WEDDING

Before I was released from the hospital, I found out that my brother's beautiful daughter, Deanna, had announced her wedding. I desperately wanted to attend. All of our family would be there, and many would be coming from different states. I had to have a cast put over the cast that I already had. They asked me what color of cast that I wanted. I told them black, so if my pants did not fit, I could put a slit in the seam and the black would hide it. It was quite a risk to attend, because I was forbidden to even touch my toe to the floor. I also had a port to take my antibiotics and for clotting factor. It took several hours for the medicine to be administered, but all of the effort was worth it, because, in my heart, I wanted to be at the wedding.

The day of the wedding arrived. I arrived in a wheelchair, with my leg propped up on a pillow. It was an extremely hot day, with the temperature soaring to 105°. I was sweating profusely. When the pictures were being taken by the photographer, he had no way of knowing what my physical situation was. With everything that was going on, we had not explained it to him. In order to be in the picture, I stood up on crutches, even though I was not supposed to let my foot touch the floor. When I got up, the photographer suddenly took the crutch away. David quickly came to my rescue, and said, "That's okay, Brother, just hold on to me." I was not able to stand very long, but they were able to get the picture taken. We only stayed briefly at the reception, because my port was getting soaked. I was so sick, not realizing at that time that I had an infection in my leg. I felt so grateful that I had been able to attend the wedding and spend time with everyone. When I see the pictures of that day, I think of my brother coming to my rescue and holding me up...like he has done so many times since.

It wasn't until later that year, in November, that the surgeon was able to put a larger prosthesis in my left leg. With much prayer, and God intervening, I hoped that I was finally done with surgeries.

However, a few months later, I was sitting on our couch and tried to get up. As I did, my right leg snapped, and, again, I was rushed to the orthopedic surgeon. After an x-ray, the surgeon told me that he would have to do another surgery on my right leg. At this point, I was completely bedridden, and was told not to bear weight on either leg. I had to wait a few more months for surgery on my right leg.

In 2006, I desperately wanted to give Mom and Dad a surprise 50th anniversary party. You have to understand, this was prior to my surgery, and I was still bedridden at this time. I needed to make all the plans for the party from my bed, and do everything in secrecy. This was almost an impossible feat, because Mom and Dad were home with me most of the time. I was able to contact over fifty people in secrecy. I would call people when Mom and Dad would go to the store or run errands. I would use any excuse I could just to get a few moments alone so that I could make calls and put together the necessary arrangements.

The party was to be held at the home of my newly married niece and her husband. My niece's husband performed the nearly impossible task of getting me down the steps and into the car so gingerly. Somehow, we were able to pull it all off. David told Mom and Dad that he was taking them out for dinner at a fancy restaurant to celebrate their anniversary, but needed to stop by Deanna's house for a minute. It was quite an ordeal. needless to say. Mom and Dad were quite surprised by the party, and were very impressed that Andy was able to get me to his home. He was even able to get me to the bathroom. The party was a huge success. Family members and friends came from different parts of Missouri, and my Aunt Sylvia even came from Tennessee.

When Dad saw our old friend, Dr. Bouhasin, at the party, he was deeply touched. Scott, who at the time was the fiancé of my niece, Crystal, made a professional looking video of the evening, and did an amazing job.

Since surgery was scheduled the next morning, Mom and Dad brought home the gifts to open later. I was not able to stay very long at the party. Early the next day, just as we were leaving to go to the hospital, Dad told Mom that they should open just one gift, and, wouldn't you know it, that one gift was a porcelain statue of a rainbow. Again, how many ways can God show a rainbow to my mother?

When I got to the hospital, they took my potassium, and it was very low at 2.2. If they would have performed surgery, I would have died on the table. The normal range is 3.5 to 5.5. They released me that day to come home.

We stopped by Dr. Mark Scheperle's office, who was my primary doctor. He had taken over my case after I could no longer see Dr. Bouhasin when I was 19. He truly knows my health situation, and sees the whole picture. He is so very caring. He was upset because they released me to come home. He said, "Why didn't they put you in the intensive care until they were able to get your potassium up to normal levels?"

Instead, my surgery was canceled and rescheduled. In the meantime, I was in agony, waiting for those two weeks until they could perform the surgery on my right leg. I was still bedridden. This last trial had been so different for me, as the Lord told us to trust in Him.

CHAPTER 20

COMPLETE TRUST IN GOD

The surgeon was able to put in another prosthesis, which was the miracle that we had asked for, and there was no infection, which was yet another miracle. No surgeon had wanted to attempt the surgery, as 95% of the bone was destroyed, due to staph infection. Each surgeon said it was impossible to put in another prosthesis. All the surgeons wanted to do amputation, except for this one surgeon who performed the surgery. When the surgery was over, the surgeon came down and told me and Dad that he put in another prosthesis. He told us that he did his very best, but he was concerned that the tibia, or the shinbone, had not healed since the surgery performed on me in June. The surgeon had purposely sliced bone in order to remove the old prosthesis without shattering the bone. It was at that time, during the surgery in June, when a doctor lifted the fragile bone and fractured the femur, the thigh bone. This surgeon said we will take one day at a time and hope that it will work.

Our God gets all the credit. Since the bone at the tibia shinbone had not healed, the surgeon did not want me to use my leg for weight-bearing, or any kind of movement for three months. This was a little disappointing to me, until I looked at the whole picture and saw that the leg was still there. In fact, the leg looked beautiful. After the surgery in June, the leg had blisters, and looked as if it had been burned.

The surgeon remarked the following day that he could not believe that the leg was not swollen more than it was. Mom stayed at the hospital, and each day that she looked down at the leg, she wanted to kiss that foot. She stayed at the hospital with me, because, even though we had a good surgeon who was willing to listen to me, communications often broke down again at the hospital. We had to be on top of everything. The clotting factor I was desperately in need of was late by hours, and Mom was at the desk every fifteen minutes demanding action. I had to have two units of blood, and needed more due to the blood loss. It was three weeks before we came home. I won't go into all the details, but, rest assured, we know that God reigns. We are so thankful for the love and prayers that went out for me. We were once again able to witness to many people in the hospital. I didn't worry about being politically correct. I just love the Lord with all my heart, and couldn't do this without Him. What a testimony! Everyone was blessed by the work of

God during this process, and couldn't get over my attitude. What a miracle of healing on my leg. I again could not bear any weight on my leg, or touch my toe to the ground, for at least three months.

During that time, I made the statement that I felt like a race horse ready to get out and run. I remembered telling God earlier in the year, "I have been prayed for by every minister and televangelist in the world for my healing, and I don't know what else to do." Now, praise God, I was walking!

CHAPTER 21

THE FAST

I remember one day getting into the shower, talking to the Holy Spirit, and Him calling on me to fast. I asked the Holy Spirit, "How long do you want me to fast?" I did not receive an answer, but I felt in my spirit that He would let me know how long I should continue the fast. Mom was quite concerned, because I was so weak after all the surgeries. A couple of days later, in the shower, the Holy Spirit spoke to me, and said, "I want you to go on a forty-four day fast." I said, "Lord, why do you want me to go on a forty-four day fast? Jesus only fasted forty days, and Daniel fasted only forty days. Why do you want me to go on a forty-four day fast?"

At that time, I was forty-four years of age. He said, "I'm going to give back to you everything that Satan has taken, and give it back to you seven fold." I began the fast totally abstaining from food, just drinking water during this time. I said, "Lord, I want to have a closer walk with you. Teach me what you want me to learn. Open the Word to me as never before. Let me understand, as I have never understood, Your Word." That is exactly what He did. I asked Him to give me a hunger for the Lord. I asked Him to teach me during this fast, and, thereafter, give me visions and dreams, and put me on a learning journey as I have never been on before. During this forty-four day fast, every time that I would read the Word, there was a new understanding like never before. In the past, there were certain things in the Bible that I did not understand. He gave me a hunger for the His Word, and everything that I read, I began to understand. He gave me a voracious appetite for more of Him...more than I had ever had in my life.

CHAPTER 22

VISIONS AND DREAMS

I began, at that time, to have visions and dreams. I remember Mom's cousin had come for a visit in the fall of 2006. I was just beginning to walk again after my surgery, and I went to get peaches. Afterwards, Mom and her cousin were both in the kitchen peeling the peaches. I was in the family room on the couch, and something happened to me that had never happened to me before. I was sitting on the sofa, and there was no one in the room with me. I was slain in the Spirit, and I had an open vision. As I looked up at the ceiling, the ceiling parted. It was like when you go to an open theater and the curtains open. As the curtains opened, I saw the largest, most beautiful church. In fact, it was so large that I could not see one end of the church from the other. The Holy Spirit was at my side, and He said, "Come with me." As we walked up the steps to the vestibule, I heard such beautiful music. My curiosity was stirred, and I just had to know where this beautiful music was coming from.

As I walked into the foyer, I saw a gold statue in the center. It was a dove fountain, and I looked to the left and to the right, and there were golden statues of Christ. I walked into the theater-style building, and everyone was dressed in their finest attire. They all had their backs toward me, and I saw them lined up from my left, all the way down to the pulpit, where there was a small fountain. All the people were in a single-file line, as they would go to the fountain. They would lean their heads back, and get three drops. I didn't understand. He said, "Darren, the church, as you know it, is dead." He said, "They are drinking sugar water. It tastes good, but offers no substance." Everyone in the line turned to look at me. They all looked as if they were from a third world country, and they were starving to death. They were dying. The Holy Spirit took me by the hand, as we walked out of the church. We walked across the parking lot, where there was a wheat field that was ready to be harvested, but no one was there to harvest it.

It was about that time that I saw a blue haze in the shape of a hand. It was the hand of God, and I saw the hand of God move to a part of the empty field. I then saw a man dressed in blue jeans and a plaid shirt standing in the field. He had no formal training to speak, but instantly God gave him the gift to preach. As I saw the hand of God move from my left to the right, I saw a lady sit down to play a piano. She had never played the piano before, but God instantly gave her the gift to play the piano, and she did so beautifully. As God's hand moved from left to right and all over the wheat field, I saw people stand, one after the other, raising their hands in glory. As they did, God began to give them the gift of tongues, interpretation of tongues, and the gift of healing.

These were not trained preachers or teachers, but they were just ordinary people, being obedient to God, as He gave them their gifts in the Holy Spirit. There are many so called Christians that have attended church their whole lives, and been raised on the pews, but they are spiritually dead.

I believe the next move of the Holy Spirit in the church will be to ordinary people who are just willing to be obedient. I believe through these people, there will be miracles untold, miracles like we have only heard about, but they have yet to be seen. I'm talking about re-creative miracles, such as limbs being regrown, eyes that are blind being restored, and eardrums being reformed. There will be gifts of tongues and interpretation of tongues.

It was during the time, after I had this open vision and had such a hunger to read the Word and understand it as I never had before, that I began to have spiritual dreams. In fact, I had seven dreams in seven nights. I remember vividly one dream about my niece, Crystal. Satan had hold of one of her arms and I had hold of the other. I was wrestling for her soul. I can remember waking up, and sitting up straight in bed. I had broken out in a sweat fighting Satan for her soul. Crystal has always been so close to my heart, and I pray for her soul each and every night.

Another dream that was so vivid to me was a dream where I felt the presence of God. I could not look at His face... I knew that if I did look upon His face, my body could not live. I had my hands on a rope, and the other end was in God's hands. I kept pulling closer and closer to God. Part of me knew that if I got too close to God, my body could not exist. I heard a voice saying, "This is Jesus, my Son, in whom I am well pleased."

I felt love as I had never felt before. The most amazing part was that I heard the voice of God saying, "This is the Holy Spirit," and it was more than I could bear. I wanted to get closer to the Holy Spirit. I felt so close to the Holy Spirit in that dream. To this day, I cannot talk about it without crying. I was so close that I could actually taste His perfume on my tongue. It was so sweet, so precious, and so tender that words cannot explain. I wish that I could explain it in words that you could understand, but there are no words to explain the experience that I had that night. This was the seventh night, and it was a night that I will never forget. However, I can say that it changed my life forever.

After those dreams, I was drawn closer to God than ever before. I remember one night, I was watching Perry Stone's program on television. After the program ended, I began to pray and seek God's face, and worship the Lord and worship the Holy Spirit. I wanted that experience once again. I wanted to taste that perfume. I remember what seemed to be most likely an hour of prayer and worship, that something amazing happened to me. My stomach began to quiver, and my jaws began to shake. I did not know what was happening to me, at first, when my jaw began to quiver. I knew I didn't have a fever. I wondered, in my natural mind, what was happening. Then I began to speak, first, in an unknown tongue, and then I began to recognize the words in Hebrew. The reason that I knew it was Hebrew is because I had spent so much time in the Word. I had no control over the quivering in my stomach, but the words came to me, "Out of your belly shall flow rivers of living water." It was an experience that I will never forget, and it lasted for a period of about two hours.

Another dream I had, while in the hospital, goes back to the year 2005, on the day that I saw the double rainbow over the hospital. I remember vividly that it happened after taking a brief fifteen minute nap. The reason I remember it is so clearly is that, during this time, I was in much pain, I could only sleep for a few minutes at a time. In that dream, I saw a picture of heaven, and it wasn't just one place. There were many earths, meaning, there were planets assigned to each and every person. To me, it meant that we were not just going to have mansions assigned to us, but we were each going to have individual planets. I know this sounds far out, but it was so real and so powerful. We were able to jump from planet to planet, instead of just mansion to mansion. I know without a doubt that heaven is going to be beyond our wildest dreams. The Word says that "eyes have not seen, nor ears heard, neither has it entered into the heart of man" what heaven, the third heaven, the place where we are going to spend eternity is going to be like. I believe that I was given a glimpse, just a small glimmer, of what Heaven is actually going to be like, and I can hardly wait to be there!

CHAPTER 23

EARTHQUAKE DREAM

It was a troubling night when I had a vivid dream about an earthquake that started in the upper suburbs of Virginia. The area was destroyed, all the way up through New York and out through Long Island. I saw it totally destroyed. The White House had totally fallen, as well as the Washington Monument and the Lincoln Memorial. Gas pipes had ruptured and everything was ablaze. I have heard it said that there is no way an earthquake could hit Washington, D.C., as well as New York, but I am telling you what I saw in my vision and it was so real and so clear. It was so real that I know it's going to happen.

I had another dream that I walked out my front door, and there was a hurricane. I could see bicycles and parts of houses flying around me, but as I looked up into the sky, it was clear and blue. I heard the Holy Spirit say to me, "Darren, you are right where I want you... in the palm of My hand." That is how I was feeling, because my life was falling apart, and yet God was totally in control. He gave me peace in the midst of the storm.

CHAPTER 24

ANGELS UNAWARE

It is written in God's Word that we should be careful, for we could entertain angels unaware. I believe that this happened to me a few years ago. It was after the time that I was on the fast for forty-four days, and I was having visions and dreams.

As I have stated before, I am a car nut and very protective of my car. When I needed service on my car, I would always go back to the mechanic and oversee what they were doing. Instead, this time, there was a black gentleman in the waiting area, and I felt drawn to stay and talk to him. Ordinarily, I would not have done so, because he looked like he was a homeless man off the streets. He smelled of urine, and his clothes were tattered. We began to talk about church, and I began to tell him my testimony. I shared with him about God, and all that He has done in my life. He just kept staring at me, and it seemed like I was doing most of the talking for almost an hour. Finally, with the biggest smile on his face, glowing with a heavenly glow, he finally spoke. He paid me the biggest compliment that anyone can pay another Christian. He said these words, "I see Jesus all over you." Even though he seemed like a homeless man from his outward appearance, like a man who was living in total poverty, he had such a glow about him.

It was about that time that they called my name to pick up my keys at the service counter. They called him at the same time, so he was standing right behind me in line at the service counter. Now here's where it gets interesting. When I picked up my keys, another person was waiting on him. There was about fifty feet between the service counter and the front door. As I picked up my keys to leave, I turned to look and see where he was, because I had my eyes on him almost the entire time. All of a sudden, I looked and he had disappeared. I thought to myself, there's no way that he could have gotten to the door that fast, so I looked in the parking lot to see if he was getting in his car. He had completely disappeared in an instant. Then I knew that I had just entertained an angel for an hour, and I knew that I had just been given a message by that angel that I truly needed at that time.

I know that the word is true that says we shall entertain angels unaware. There is absolutely no way that man could have gotten out of my sight that quickly without me seeing him leave. It was a message from God sent by an angel from heaven to encourage me. Be careful who you speak with, because that person might just be an angel sent by God to talk to you and minister to you in your hour of need.

CHAPTER 25

ANOTHER WEDDING

I was feeling so much better in the year 2007, and was getting excited to get out of the house. When my niece, Crystal, asked me to sing "The Lord's Prayer" at her wedding, I immediately agreed. Even though I was still weak, I wanted desperately to be there, and see her in her beautiful wedding gown. Our family came from out of state, as well as many parts of Missouri. I, of course, wanted to be a part of the celebration, as well.

On July 7, 2007, I attended her wedding, and did, in fact, sing "The Lord's Prayer"...as she had requested. I was barely able to stand, but with God's help, I was able to attend Crystal's wedding and celebrate her special day.

CHAPTER 26

THE NEW CAR

Mom and Dad were looking for a new car. We found a 2005 Cadillac that only had 7,000 miles on it. It was silver in color and was loaded, with all the bells and whistles. It was a beautiful car. Mom wasn't sure about the idea of buying the car, because she said that it looked too plain. I told her not to worry about it, that she just needed to give me two weeks and I would have it looking beautiful.

I was walking quite well during that time, and was able to do the work myself. I put extra chrome on the bottom and on the top of the car. I put extra wood appliqués on the car, as well. I also put a black roof on the silver car. She fell in love with it. I wanted to get all of this work done on the car in time for our upcoming family reunion

with all of Mom's six sisters. I wanted her to be proud of her new car. We had rented a condo right on the beach in Gulf Shores, Alabama. I had spent over two weeks working on that car, to get it ready for my mom. My brother said that he thought something was going to happen to it, because the car looked too perfect.

CHAPTER 27

THE FARM

About this same time, in 2007, Dad sold his great love...his farm. The farm was where he had grown up. As we were loading the remaining furniture, the trailer hitch full of furniture fell on David's hand and broke it. Without even hesitating, Dad tried to lift the trailer hitch off of David's hand. Immediately, Dad felt something snap around his heart, but he didn't say anything to us about what he had felt. He had already started having periodic chest pains. The farm had been his place to get away, and to get release from the stress and noise of the city. He loved to get out of town and he loved nature. He worked hard, but when he would get to the farm, he would just sit out on the porch and listen to the whippoorwill and the quietness of the country.

He also had an organ down at the farm, and would play it when he came in from working in the garden that he had planted. I had never seen him grieve as much as he did when he sold the farm.

We left in two different trucks loaded with the items from the farm to head back home. David and I were in one truck, and dad was in the other truck. We couldn't figure out why Dad was so far behind us until we got home to St. Louis. He later explained that he had walked into the woods one last time, reliving precious memories in his mind, knowing that he would not be able to return to the place that he loved so much. He was not able to work like he used to, and was, unfortunately, facing the reality that his life was changing. His heart was broken.

CHAPTER 28

THE CAR ACCIDENT

A few months later, it was time for us to leave for our family reunion at Gulf Shores, Alabama. We were excited for the upcoming trip, and excited to get to see our family. As we drove through Nashville, I was enjoying our new car, and admiring how it handled on the road. I was proud of the work that I had been able to accomplish on the car.

When we got through Nashville, Dad told me that he would like to drive. We stopped to get a sandwich and change drivers at that time. We had not driven but a couple of miles when we came upon a wreck. Traffic was at a complete stop. It was at this time, at exactly 11:32 a.m., Central Time, when four out of six of Mom's sisters felt in their spirit that they were to pray for us.

Mom's sister, Shirley, who lives in Florida, said to her husband at exactly 12:32 p.m., Eastern Time, "I feel led to pray for Louise, Jewell Dee, and Darren. I want to pray that God will give them traveling mercies as they travel." My Aunt Bessie and Aunt Frances were in Alabama, and were on the phone discussing recipes that they would prepare for our visit. They stopped immediately at 11:32 a.m., Central Time, and said, "Let's pray for Louise, Jewell Dee, and Darren as they travel today." Mary, Mom's other sister, who we call the comedian of the group, but who is also someone very close to God, said the Lord spoke to her. He said, "If you don't stop now, and pray for Louise, you will never see her again." This was also exactly at 11:32 a.m., Central Time. Mom's baby sister, Wanda, also had a burden to pray for us.

When we were at a complete stop on the highway, held up by the traffic accident, we had no idea what was about to happen. All of a sudden, a tractor-trailer, going about 60 miles an hour, came off an interchange. He never touched his brakes. He hit another tractor-trailer in front of him, which, in turn, hit a pickup truck. The pickup truck hit us, knocking our car so that it was going completely the other direction on the highway. We were the only people involved in the accident that were not taken away in an ambulance. After the accident, Dad began to have chest pains, and began to take his nitroglycerin. Mom began to travail in prayer. I grabbed my camera in one hand and my telephone in the other, calling 911, and at the same time snapping pictures of the accident for evidence. I also was doing a triage of the people behind us that were thrown out of their cars on the highway.

In short, only by the grace of God, were we spared from certain death. If we had been hit directly by the tractor-trailer, who never even hit his brakes, we would have been instantly killed.

I did not know this at the time because my adrenaline was still pumping from the accident, but my left elbow, which was already in such bad shape from all of the years of hemorrhaging, had hit the dashboard during the accident.

The State Highway Patrol advised us that we should not drive the car in its current condition. We were going to go to the next exit to see if we could rent a car to continue our journey on to Gulf Shores. We could not get off at that exit, because there was another accident in front of us. The car involved was flipped over on its top.

Our car was severely damaged, but it was still drivable, so we continued on. About ten minutes later, I began to feel the hemorrhage in my left elbow. We got off at the next exit and pulled into a Steak 'n Shake parking lot, and I got my clotting factor out of the car. About that time, my phone rang. It was my cousin, Kenny. He said, "I was just thinking about you. Are you okay?" I told him about the accident, while I was taking my clotting factor.

For those couple of days that we were there at the condo, I could not get my elbow to stop bleeding. What I didn't realize was that this was not a simple hemorrhage. During the accident, the bones in my left elbow were crushed, severely damaging it beyond repair.

After we got home to St. Louis, I had my elbow x-rayed, confirming what I already knew. Something was horrifically wrong...my elbow was crushed. I had gone several days, gritting my way through the pain.

Mom's back was also injured during the accident. She had been sitting in the backseat, Had we not had the trunk full of luggage, which I believe absorbed a lot of the impact, she could have been severely injured. The beautiful new car that I had worked on so hard received about $11,000 worth of damage, but at least it was repairable.

I began to look for a new doctor over the next several months that would be willing to do something about my elbow. All of this happened in October of 2007.

CHAPTER 29

ELBOW SURGERY

It wasn't until May of 2008, after seeing doctor after doctor that stated that there was nothing that they could do for my elbow, that I finally found an orthopedic surgeon. He looked at my left hand, my pinky, and my ring finger. They had begun to turn black. The orthopedic surgeon said, "Darren, I have to replace your elbow, because you have lost the blood flow to your pinky and your ring finger. If I don't do something quickly, I'll have to amputate your left arm from just above your elbow." I am left-handed...this was my left arm. This would have been devastating to me. The surgeon was booked for several months, but he had his nurse book an emergency surgery for me for the month of May.

Prior to my surgery in January of 2008, Dad had to have emergency open heart surgery. Dad's heart was blocked 100% in three of the arteries in the front of the heart, and blocked 60% in the arteries in the back of his heart. He was taking approximately 100 nitroglycerin a week, just to stay alive. Dad had the open heart surgery, which he did not want to do. We were fortunate to find a wonderful surgeon who performed the surgery on him.

A few months later, I had the surgery on my left elbow to put in a prosthesis. I had no idea how extensive the damage to my elbow was, and what the surgery would involve. I had blisters the size of coffee cans on my arm. When we went back in a week after the surgery, I had a bleed in my elbow so severe that when the doctor tried to aspirate it, he hit an open blood vessel. It was a

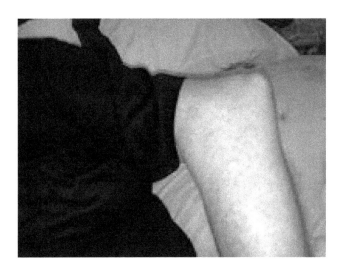

catastrophe. He took a tarp to catch the blood and his eyes bulged with fright, but he then sent us home instead of sending us to the emergency room. It was a miracle that I didn't bleed to death since it was another hour getting home. Mom ran into the house and prepared a double dose of clotting factor, which I took every twelve hours for days, to stop the hemorrhage.

After I had my elbow replaced, I had hoped things were going to get better. It was now 2009. Dad had spent many months on the computer, looking for a new truck. That was something he had never done. He had always bought a truck off the lot, but this time he was going to order the truck of his dreams. I was doing the same thing, as well. I was ordering the car of my dreams. On the day that we went to pick up Dad's truck, I got a phone call from a car dealer in Illinois, who was located about 140 miles from St. Louis.

The dealer had found the exact model that I was looking for and had been wanting to order. Dad drove his new truck home that day with a smile on his face, and it was beautiful!

The next day, we took the trip to pick up my car at the dealership in Illinois. With all the cars that I had owned, I had never driven a car off the showroom floor. I wasn't feeling very well, but I tried to shake it off as being the excitement about my car.

CHAPTER 30

FEELING THE DEATH ANGEL

After arriving home after picking up my car, I started to run a high fever. The next day I went to my primary physician, but he was not available, so I saw the nurse practitioner. She swabbed my nose, and assured me it wasn't the H1N1 flu, but just a virus. I told her I had sharp pain in my side. She passed it off, as did I. Later that evening, I developed a fever of 105°. Dad started bringing up pots of hot water and putting towels over my head. It was getting harder and more difficult to breathe in and out. Finally, the time had come... Mom called the doctor's office and told them that they were going to take me to the emergency room. I was rushed to the hospital. When they took the x-ray, they saw that I had double pneumonia, and my lungs were completely filled with fluid. They put me in isolation, and made anyone that entered the room wear masks, gowns, and caps on their heads.

I knew I was dying before I left the house. I could feel the death angel. I felt as if I was at the bottom of the pool. I could not breathe in or out. I was praying for the strength of God to help me live. They told me at the hospital as they were giving me breathing treatments, that I had indeed almost died.

Prior to the time that I was admitted to the hospital with pneumonia, Dad began to trip up the steps while we were at the house. He began running over the trash cans in the driveway, and he stumbled over the steps getting into the house. He didn't know it, but he was having small strokes. He tried to shake it off as if nothing was wrong, but I knew better. It was also about this time that Mom had to have surgery on her shoulder to repair a torn rotator cuff, so Dad was trying to take care of both Mom and me.

I was released from the hospital about a week later after my bout with pneumonia, and then it happened…

CHAPTER 31

THE LOSS OF MY BEST FRIEND

My dad was not only my best friend, but he was my buddy and confidante. He was a mechanic, a carpenter, a plumber, an electrician, a cook, a tailor and a designer. He was a jack-of-all-trades. There was nothing that he could not do and did not do. In fact, he built the house where we currently reside, in 1965. He taught me everything that I know, and I hung on his heels all of my life.

On November 1, 2009, Dad had gone to the store to get the ingredients to make chicken casserole, which was his favorite recipe. At that time, Mom was in therapy with her shoulder after rotator cuff surgery. Dad helped Mom prepare the casserole, as it was hard for her to pick things up, and on that evening we enjoyed his favorite dish.

Dad's routine was to get up every morning, get dressed about 5 a.m., and go to the doughnut shop...not to eat doughnuts, but to talk to the boys and drink coffee for about an hour.

The next morning, I heard him go into the bedroom to get his clothes on. I thought that he had left for the doughnut shop, so I went back to sleep. Mom was still sleeping, as well. When she woke up, she looked out the window, saw Dad's truck, and thought he had returned from the doughnut shop. She decided to try to get dressed by herself that morning, without bothering Dad and took her time getting dressed. When she came downstairs at 8:30 a.m., I heard her scream, "Darren, I can't get Dad awake." He had never gotten dressed, or gone to the doughnut shop.

He had come downstairs and was lying on the couch in a coma, barely able to breathe. I turned him on his side, so that he wouldn't choke, and immediately called 911. They arrived within two minutes, and took him to the closest hospital, which is about ten minutes away from our house. The doctor told David and me that Dad had suffered a massive stroke. He said, "We are going to try to operate, but it's in his brain stem and I don't know if he will survive." Dad went into a deep coma. They told David and me that Dad would not survive. Even if he did, he would be blind and deaf, and totally paralyzed on his right side. His temperature soared to 109°. They kept him on ice for the three days that he was in a deep coma. He never recovered.

My dad was blessed to be given the talent to play the organ more beautifully than anyone you have ever heard. It was a God-given gift. He could play so many instruments. They always say that you can destroy the mind, but never the soul. Mom was so devastated losing the love of her life. Never in a million years did she imagine Dad going before her. This happened so suddenly, and Mom felt there was no closure. Because of the coma, there had not been a chance to tell Dad how much he meant to her.

As I mentioned before, I had almost died with pneumonia, and Mom had just had shoulder surgery. Dad had been tirelessly and selflessly taking care of us, all the while dealing with so many critical health issues of his own.

The night before they were scheduled to disconnect Dad from life support, Mom cried out to God. She prayed. "Dear Lord, intervene and send an angel in the morning, either at the hospital or show up some way to tell me everything will be ok." When Mom and I arrived at the hospital the next morning, a nurse asked Mom to walk down the hall with her. She said these words, "As I entered your husband's room this morning, about 6 a.m., I felt the presence of the Holy Spirit so strong that goose bumps ran all over me." Mom told the nurse that she was the angel that she had prayed for.

Mom had a cassette tape that Dad had made years earlier of him playing the organ at the farm. That was the only tape in existence. She had looked through all the drawers about ten times, trying to locate the cassette tape, but was unable to find it. Then, as we were walking out the door that final day with Dad, she looked one last time, and found the tape. We took a cassette tape player and laid it on his bedside. The doctors and nurses said we could take our time saying our last goodbyes.

The room was filled with family members. We gathered together, and as the tape played Dad's songs, we sang and raised our hands towards Heaven and praised the Lord for over an hour. David, Mom and I witnessed Dad's countenance change as we worshiped in song. I didn't know if I should lay my hands on Dad and rebuke the spirit of death, but I was checked in my spirit, as I knew he would not want to live life in a vegetative state. Our only closure was that he had such a look of peace on his face. At exactly 11:05 a.m., on November 5, 2009, at the age of 75 years old, my father stepped out of this life and went to be with Jesus. It is a day I will never forget. I remember when they disconnected him from life support, I put my fingers on his carotid artery. I could feel his pulse growing weaker and weaker. I looked at my watch and saw that at 11:05 a.m. His heart had completely stopped. He took his final breath here on earth, and his first breath in heaven.

CHAPTER 32

HONORING MY DAD

By the number of people who came for the visitation at the funeral home, you would have thought Dad was a rock star. People were lined up out the door, just to come in and pay their last respects. He was so loved! I was still so weak from the double pneumonia that I was as white as a sheet. I told Mom that I wished our dear friend, Dr. Debra Peppers, could have been there, but she was a thousand miles away in Florida. I was talking to family and friends at the back of the funeral home, and I said, "Mom, look!" To my surprise, there was Deborah Peppers. She came over to Mom, and said that the Holy Spirit told her that she had to come. She asked me to start singing the song, "The Anchor Holds." Mom told her that I was so weak that I could hardly stand, much less sing, but she looked at me and said, "Darren, start singing." I would have done anything for her. She is so special to me. I began to sing the first verse, and, instead of the normal mourning at a funeral, it was like a prayer meeting. One moment there was naturally tears of sadness, but then there were great moments of rejoicing. We all knew that Dad had stepped into heaven exactly the way that he wanted to. He could not have handled living life in a vegetative state.

Dad always had a sense of humor and was always joking around. When he had the farm, if he said this once, he said it a hundred times, "If anything happens to me, don't ever put me in a nursing home, just tie me to a tree and let the dogs have me." A lot of people may find that funny, but he was serious. He could never have handled being in a nursing home.

Up until he had his heart surgery, he had never been to a doctor. He was a giant among men, and he can never be replaced. I've had many dreams about Dad since he died. One that I remember, specifically, was that I was in a building and I could not find the exit. Every time I went down the hall, the door was locked. All of a sudden, I looked over my left shoulder and I saw Dad at my side. He didn't look as he did when he had died. He had a full head of curly black hair, just like he did when he was thirty years old. He was dressed in a red sweater and black pants, and he said, "What's wrong, Babe?" He would always call me Babe. I said, "Dad, I can't find the way out of here. I'm trying to find my way to my car." He looked at me with those loving and compassionate eyes of his, and softly said to me, as he took my hand, "That's okay, Babe, come with me, and I'll show you the way out of here." I believe the way Dad looked in my dream is the way he looks in heaven now, with a new glorified body...a body with no heart problems, with no effects from a stroke. I believe that we are going to look like we are around the age of thirty in heaven, around the age Jesus was when he died on the cross.

I miss my dad so very much. It's been nine years since his death, and yet, selfishly, there are times when I want him back. I know that he is so happy now, though, and that he would never want to come back. For that, I am eternally grateful. I will see you soon, Dad, I will see you soon. I love you, and I can't wait to see you at the gates of Heaven. I can't wait until the day that I enter the pearly gates, and I hear dad playing the organ so beautifully.

He made the statement many years ago, "I would rather play the organ than to eat when I'm hungry." He had the most beautiful touch, and he could make an organ "talk". He will never be able to be replaced and he will never be forgotten, not by me and not by anyone who knew him. He was that kind of man. You had to know him to know what I am talking about. He was the life of the party. Anyone who talked to him for more than five minutes instantly fell in love with him. I had the privilege of having him as my Dad for forty-seven years. I'll see you soon, my friend, I'll see you soon. I can hardly wait for that day.

CHAPTER 33

HONORING MY MOM

What can I say about my mom? Most people can say they love their mother, but I can tell you from 56 years of being in her wonderful presence, that I have a saint for a mom. I can tell you from personal experience that I have never heard a foul word or a mean thing come out of her mouth. She has her devotional time in the evening with the Lord, and spends time reading the Word.

She then comes down to the side of my bed, where I have been bedridden since 2010, and we will join hands in prayer and supplication. We bring each member of the family before God for their soul, and pray that none be lost. I have never seen anyone nearer to God than my mother. I have grown closer to her since the passing of my dad, closer than ever before. I cannot begin to tell my mom how much I love her and respect her. She is a queen among women, a woman who is much to be admired, as a precious stone. I love her so!

CHAPTER 34

THE START OF A LONG NIGHTMARE

During the passing of my dad, I was falling constantly. In fact, on the day that they disconnected him from life support, I fell four times in the hallway and in the parking lot. I knew that my leg was getting worse. There was so much going on at that time. My elbow, that had been replaced, was failing two months after the passing of my father. It was a cold day in January when I had to go back to the hospital for more surgery. Doctors attempted to fix the ulnar nerve in my elbow, but unfortunately, it failed to fix the problem.

I continued to fall, so I went back to my orthopedic surgeon. He found a big knot, about the size of a baseball, just below my kneecap. As I asked the orthopedic surgeon if he was afraid to

tackle this problem and to fix it, he said, "Yes, Darren, this is not my area of expertise." He suggested two options. He gave me two locations of hospitals where I could go, and get the problem fixed. One was in Nashville, Tennessee, and the other was in Minnesota. We chose Nashville.

CHAPTER 35

NASHVILLE SURGERY

Nashville seemed like the perfect location for my surgery, because we had a precious angel close by. My mom's sister, Sylvia, lived in Nashville. She took us into her home for over seven weeks. She did everything for us, even cooked and cleaned. When I went to the hospital, she brought a blowup mattress, so that Mom would have a place to sleep at my bedside. We are eternally grateful for everything she did for us.

We first went for a consultation with the orthopedic surgeon, then surgery was scheduled at Vanderbilt Hospital. We again traveled to Nashville for a second consultation in April. My surgery was scheduled for early in July of 2010. I was worried about taking the journey from St. Louis back to Nashville during the Fourth of July weekend, because of the hectic traffic, but we didn't have a choice. I was quickly getting worse.

They opened up my knee and removed the pseudo-tumor, which had grown to the size of a softball and had turned black. They took the calf muscle of my left leg, and reversed the skin and muscle to cover the huge hole that was left after they removed the tumor. Thank God, the tumor was benign. The reason why I had been continuously falling was that the tumor had eaten away half of my kneecap. I kept thinking to myself, "Why did the doctors wait so long to do the surgery?" Maybe if the surgery had been performed earlier, they could have averted all this damage. They were unaware, however, of the detriment taking place.

After the muscle flap was completed, I began to develop giant hematomas. One was so large that you could fit a Pepsi can down into the hole. They also installed a port into my chest to put the medication in. The port became infected and I got a staff infection. I remember vividly, one afternoon, while we were staying at Aunt Sylvia's house, I had a follow-up visit. As I was starting to get into the car to go to the follow-up visit, one of the large hematomas burst, and it bled all over the driveway. There was probably half a gallon of blood and pus. It was bleeding so profusely that I could not get back into the house. I had to attend to my wound, in the garage of Aunt Sylvia's house, in 100° heat.

I then drove to my appointment, and the plastic surgeon packed the hole with a patch. We hoped it would work, but, instead, the patch also became infected with a staff infection. Later that evening, I began to run a high fever and began vomiting. Early the next morning, we had to call an ambulance, and I was rushed to the emergency room at Vanderbilt Hospital. Staff was called in from Orthopedics, Plastic Surgery, and Hematology. Everyone was very concerned. Once again, I was admitted to the hospital, and a debridement was performed.

When Mom saw the hole, she almost fainted. They began to pack the hole with strips of a cotton-like substance, dipped in medication, to try to get the hole closed. I was a very unusual case.

With so many surgeries in Nashville, my mother was well-acquainted with the constant waiting. While I was in surgery, my aunt made the comment that Mom must have a waiting room ministry. She would witness to the many hurting people with devastating needs in the waiting room, and would pray with them. On one occasion, she witnessed to a lovely couple whose nephew was having brain surgery. She shared about God giving the sign of the rainbow to her on so many occasions.

The next morning, this couple found my room, and gave Mom a packet of rainbow seeds. It was the most unusual thing Mom had ever seen. The sealed packet of rainbow seeds had a poem on it with rainbow blessings. They said that they had this packet of seeds for ten years and had started to throw it away, but felt led that day to bring it with them. After hearing Mom's story, they gave it to her.

Since the port had become infected, I had to have it removed. I had become septic, and had to wait to have a new port reinstalled. This was a hectic time for all of my family, because I was so very sick.

In the meantime, my brother, David, had been transferred from St. Louis to Dallas, Texas, in order to keep his job at American Airlines. He would take his days off to come to visit me in the hospital. The wound finally closed, after several weeks, and we were allowed to go home. David took his day off to drive us home from Nashville back to St. Louis.

When I got home, new hematomas continued to pop up. When the hematomas would burst, the blood vessels would break, sounding like popping balloons. The blood would shoot across the room, along with huge blood clots. I would have to turn my knee over, and let the blood drain like a fountain into a basin. This was a recurring nightmare, as I would work for weeks at a time to try to get the hematomas to close. After one would close, a new one would come up in its place. It would eventually burst, starting the process all over again. It seemed like it was every week that we had to call paramedics to rush me to the hospital in St. Louis.

There was no way to go back to Vanderbilt Hospital, in Nashville, with me bleeding so severely. At St. Luke's Hospital, I had a plastic surgeon that scheduled me for surgery on Good Friday, April 22, 2011. I remember this vividly. They were wheeling me down for the surgery, and a tornado hit St. Louis. Surgery should have been canceled. I remarked to the surgeon, "What will you do if we lose power?" He stated that they had generators for backup. St. Louis was indeed hit, but God brought me through once again.

I have to thank all of the doctors who have worked on me, from plastic surgeons to infectious disease doctors. They have all tried so hard to make life better for me. However, many times there were doctors who didn't want to have to deal with me and my situation.

It was Christmas time when we again called 911. After being transferred to St. Luke's Hospital, they told me that I needed to go St. Louis University Hospital. They transferred me there without even notifying my primary. After being examined at St. Louis University Hospital, they asked me why I didn't go back to Nashville. They didn't want me either. I remember Mom saying, "I feel like Jesus, when they said, 'There is no room at the inn."

The doctors asked Mom if she would write about my history, and all the surgeries, as I was such an unusual case. They would study all night, learning something about this unusual case. We were discharged. Our orthopedic surgeon, in Nashville, was called, who then scheduled yet another debridement surgery. After the surgery, the surgeon made the statement that if we should ever return, it would only be to amputate the leg. This was yet another closed door.

After a few months, my elbow, that had been replaced in 2008, had started to come apart. We made an appointment with the surgeon that had performed the surgery in St. Louis. The surgeon was reluctant, as it was very high risk to ever do another replacement. He feared I might lose the use of my arm. However, he scheduled surgery, in spite of his reluctance, due to the prosthesis coming apart.

After being in the hospital, the surgeon found infection in my bladder. He thought the infection was coming from my leg. He refused to ever do surgery on my elbow again. The bone in my elbow was sticking out, and I was in terrible agony. I would try to lie on my side, and pull it back in place each night.

We then sought out two more surgeons to do the elbow, but both sternly refused. My options were running out, and I began to look at surgeons located out of state. I had no way to get there. and if I could somehow find a way, they most likely would also refuse to perform the surgery. I had to live with this situation, while dealing with so many other issues. I was living a nightmare constantly, over and over again. What would we do without Jesus saying to us that He'll do it again? It is like the song I have sung so many times, that says, "He'll Do It Again." He will do it again, and will bring healing and deliverance.

The journey continued, as we sought out new doctors, time and again. I began vomiting twenty-five to thirty times a day, and no one ever discovered why. I was scheduled for vascular surgery for the bleeding in my hematomas in my leg. I feared the surgery would not take place, as I was so sick, but the surgeon stated, "I will knock you out, and you will stop vomiting."

At Barnes Hospital, as we were getting scheduled for yet another surgery, the surgeon opened up my leg. It was so vascular, which means the amount of blood vessels were so numerous, there was no way to tie off all of the blood vessels. He closed the leg, and said, "There is nothing I can do." He showed us pictures of how vascular it was, and had no good news for me. Yet again, we faced another disappointment.

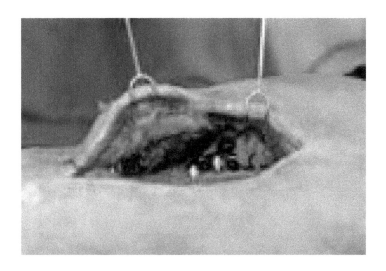

A beautiful lady, that worked as a concierge, found out that we had checked in for surgery that day. She came in, and started talking to us. As we were sharing our story, she said, "I thought about you two, as I was baking a cake for a special person to lift their spirits." She showed us a picture of the cake. As it was cut, the layers were the colors of the rainbow. Mom cried again, saying, "How many ways God reveals to me the rainbow." We held on to the covenant of the rainbow, even though our hearts were discouraged.

CHAPTER 36

MORE HOSPITALS

Changing the dressings so many times a day and losing so much blood, I became weaker and weaker. The constant vomiting grew more frequent. One day, I had vomited for many hours, and I had a fever that started to climb. Mom knew we had to get to the hospital. Somehow, we managed to get downstairs and into the car. Mom was driving, while my head was in the bucket vomiting profusely. Only God helped us during that trip to the hospital, because I was getting to the point of passing out. Mom was trying to look at me, while also trying to watch the road.

Upon arrival at the emergency room at Barnes Hospital, Mom left the car outside the emergency room doors and ran in the front door screaming, "Somebody help me." Nurses came running with a wheelchair, and got me in the emergency room. They gave me nausea shots, but were only allowed to give me a total of three. Nothing was helping or stopping the vomiting. When they drew my blood, I had a staph infection and was septic. My entire body was infected, my leg as well as my bloodstream. They gave me such a large dose of vancomycin that it shut down my kidneys. They were ready to do dialysis, but, thank God, little by little, my kidneys started to function on their own. After a few days, I was able to go home.

As I have previously said, many surgeries were scheduled in hospitals from Tennessee to St. Louis, using nuclear tests. As a last ditch effort, it was thought that radiation would work in an effort to stop the bleeding.

We found a doctor at Barnes Hospital who thought he may be able to stop the bleeding with twenty-four treatments of radiation. I was driving Mom and myself down to the treatments, and walking to the car using my crutches. Then Mom would get the wheelchair out of the car. On the day of my last treatment, as I drove in the driveway at home and reached for my crutches, I felt that something was very wrong. As I attempted to get out of the car, it was as if someone was standing on my feet. My brother was at work, so he sent my sister-in-law over to help me get out of the car. She was directly behind me. I began to fall onto the concrete porch, but she accidentally fell on top of me in her attempt to help me. You could hear my feet snap, and crack like broken twigs.

I have not walked one step since that day. Each and every time I have had doctor's appointments, we had to call the fire department to get me up out of bed and down the stairs. My brother then had to bring my bed downstairs, as the paramedics were having trouble getting me downstairs on a stretcher.

One day, as Mom and I were watching TV, we heard about a doctor who was trying a new product called MatriStem that helped fingers to grow back. We sought him out, and he agreed to take on the challenge. He tried three surgeries in January, February, and March of that year, and took skin grafts from my upper thigh to cover the hole left by the hematomas. Unfortunately, the MatriStem would not adhere to the metal. In March, I had my last skin graft, but the MatriStem just would not adhere. Every time that I had a doctor's appointment, I would try to hide the fact from the surgeon that the MatriStem was not covering the metal. I would quickly pull the skin over the metal trying to fool the surgeon. I did not want him to see that it was not working.

CHAPTER 37

THE WORST DAY OF MY LIFE

As I was in the doctor's office, expecting just a routine exam, I thought that I would hear the doctor say, "Darren we are going to try one last time." I was not expecting to hear the words that would forever change my life. He said, "Darren, I've done all I can do, but it's not working. It's not adhering to the metal and it's infected, and if I don't do something right now, we are going to lose you." The words just flew over my head, and, basically, went in one ear and out the other. I could not comprehend what he was saying. Since the doctor's office was directly across the street from the hospital, he said, "I've got to call, and get you a room right away." It was my worst nightmare. I was trying to understand what he was saying to me when he added these words, "Darren, I am sorry, but I've got to take the leg, or I am going to lose you." The words just kept ringing in my ears of the scripture that God had given me, from Proverbs 3:26, "For I the Lord shall be thy confidante, and I shall keep thy foot from being taken." I wondered how this could be happening to me. I know that God cannot lie and I had stood on that scripture for eleven years. The Lord had come through so many times...

over and over He kept me from amputation. I did not understand how this could be happening.

Surgery was scheduled for the following day, and all I could do was weep. I have never been so broken-hearted or so confused. I was in shock. I remember talking to Mom, asking her, "Mom, what have I done wrong?" She said, "Honey, you've done nothing wrong. No one has ever lived as close to God as you." We held each other as we wept. We were both numb. All I could do was to put my situation in God's hands.

The next morning, my niece, Deanna, her husband, Andy, and their precious baby, as well as David and my sister-in-law, Peggy, came to see me just to give me hugs and encourage me.

That next evening, I had several angels walk through the door. My precious longtime friend, Kim, and my Aunt Jean came to comfort me. My Aunt Sylvia and her oldest daughter, my cousin, Jennifer, came as well. They had driven all the way from Nashville to be by my side in my hour of need. My cousin, Renee, also came, with four prayer warriors, young adults, who laid on their faces for hours in prayer, praying that God would intervene. I just knew in my heart that God would intervene at the midnight hour. I could not speak to anyone. All I could do was weep, because I did not understand why God would allow this to happen. How could He allow my left leg to be amputated above the knee? That night, as I dozed off for just a few minutes, I had a dream that I was in a beautiful gray suit, standing at the pulpit in the church. My leg was completely restored, and I heard the voice of the Holy Spirit telling me that He was going to give me the gift of a healing ministry. In this dream, I was standing completely restored, with all of my prostheses laying at my side... the one from my right leg, my right shoulder, and my left elbow. I had been completely restored.

There was something more to this dream, because I was praying for the sick. More importantly, I was praying for amputees and they were all being completely healed. Why was God showing me this the night before I was about to lose my leg? I was numb in one respect, like it wasn't happening, but yet I had to face reality.

I was taken down to surgery. When the doctor began to amputate my leg, he said that my foot literally crumbled in his hand. This fulfilled the scripture from Proverbs 3:26. What I mean is that no one took my foot. It literally crumbled in his hand. If I would have stepped on it, it would've shattered like broken glass, and I would have bled to death.

As soon as I came out of the anesthesia and my eyes opened, I pulled back the sheet to see if my leg was there. To my horror, my left leg was gone. The tears began to flow, as I knew my life had changed. I was reminded of my dream, of my restored body. The Holy Spirit had told me that I was going to be in the healing ministry, praying for impossible cases...cases where bodies were fully restored. I knew that something miraculous was about to happen. God was going to give back what Satan had stolen from me.

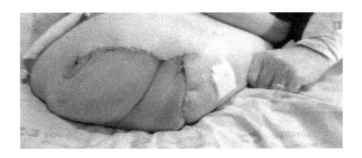

Since that time, I have had numerous dreams and visions. In my dreams, I see myself jumping out of bed, and walking on two new legs. Lying beside me are all my prostheses, my right shoulder, my left elbow, and even my right leg. They are lying beside me, and I am completely restored. I feel in my heart, and in my spirit, that God is going to give me a miraculous healing ministry, but I can't do that if my body is not perfect. I cannot wait until the day that God completes this miracle that He has started in me.

CHAPTER 38

YET ANOTHER MIRACLE

While still in shock of losing my left leg, my elbow was completely destroyed. I had been unable to see another orthopedic surgeon, as I had been dealing with my leg for so long. The surgeon that took off my leg said that I should go back and tell my orthopedic surgeon there is no risk. However, when we called the surgeon for an appointment, he told me that I would have to live with my elbow the way it was, because he would not take the risk of performing the surgery.

Mom said to him, "Can't you give us a name of another surgeon," but he replied, "No one would take your case." We felt like a revolving door, going from doctor to doctor, and never receiving good news.

We actually went to two more elbow specialists, and they also refused to perform the surgery. The third surgeon said that all he could do would be to take out the prosthesis, and put in a straight rod, leaving my arm straight. Since I am left-handed, this is my dominant arm. I told him I would not agree to that surgery.

Mom and I left his office with heavy hearts. We then heard from a friend who gave us the name of another surgeon. We made an appointment with that surgeon. We were praying for favor.

I felt like this was the hand of God moving on my behalf. It was as if we didn't have to say a word. He said, "Darren, I understand that you've had problems with different issues. Even if you have an infection, I will insert an antibiotic spacer, and leave it in for six months until the infection is cleared up." He did not hesitate to take on this severe challenge.

The surgery was to take several hours, and Mom waited and prayed. You usually receive an update every two hours. Mom received the first update, and, as she waited to get her next update, she was told that the surgeon wanted to see her in the conference room. Her heart sank, as this was usually where the surgeon meets with you to give you bad news. By that time, David had arrived at the hospital, and, as he looked at Mom, he knew what she was feeling. The surgeon came in with a smile on his face. He said that all that he had to do was half of the prosthesis, and weave the bones together with a putty-like substance, giving me back the full mobility that I had not had in nine years. The surgeon told Mom and David that everything had gone well. In fact, he said, "Everything went perfectly." I had prayed the same prayer that I had prayed with my knee years before. I had asked the Lord to send ministering angels, so that, in the event that something would go wrong, the angels would give the surgeon and his team ideas that they wouldn't ordinarily have. That is exactly what happened. The surgeon took the putty-like substance, and weaved the bones together like needle and thread.

I had to wear a cast night and day, one to keep it straight, and the other to keep it bent. One cast was for night, and the other was for day. The surgeon wanted me to do my own therapy. He said, "Darren, if you can get your thumb to your chin in the next six months, that's all we can hope for." Within six months, I could get my thumb all the way to my voice-box. I could dress myself again. I could eat normally. I could do the things that I had not been able to do in many years. I thank God for a complete miracle.

CHAPTER 39

TESTS AND MORE TESTS

The last six years have been a nightmare for me, with one thing after the other. As I stated earlier, I have had so many dreams, and so many visions of being in the healing ministry. I know I could not have gone through everything I have had to go through, if God had not shown me what the future holds.

Not only have I been in bed for the last six and half years, but it has constantly been one health issue after another. For example, shortly after my elbow was completed, I began to bleed in my bladder. I shook off my concerns at first, thinking it was caused by kidney stones. I had suffered with kidney stones about fifteen years ago. I would have as many as ten kidney stones over the course of a year. When I began to bleed in the bladder, I thought it was just another kidney stone. Did I just say JUST?

My wonderful primary doctor, Dr. Mark Scheperle, who has taken care of me for thirty years, sent me for an MRI test. After the report came back from the MRI, it showed a mass on my kidney. I was sent to a nephrologist, who specialized in kidney problems. He told me that he would have to remove my kidney because of the mass, which was a tumor on top of the kidney. He scheduled yet another MRI with dye contrast. After this MRI, this same surgeon advised me that he didn't have to remove my kidney. In fact, he told me that he didn't even need to see me again. Praise God for yet another miracle.

However, the bleeding in my bladder continued, so much so that I went to my old urologist. I had to go through several intensive tests. After those tests, surgery was scheduled to remove a tumor that they found on one kidney. The surgeon was delighted to find no cancer. Praise God, it was benign and not cancerous. The surgeon was so delighted that he called me five times at home. God had again been with me in my hour of need.

Shortly thereafter, my blood pressure began to skyrocket, and my primary doctor put me on medication. I had to go in for a CT scan, as well as another MRI. They could not find why my blood pressure was so high. They sent me to a cardiologist, who ordered a stress test, an EKG, and another MRI. I did not pass the stress test, and had to go to the hospital for a heart catheter. The surgeon came out with smiles, and told Mom there was no blockage. We were, of course, greatly relieved.

Since my blood pressure continued to be high, I had to see another surgeon who specializes in adrenal glands. He thought that this was my problem and increased my medication. He said there was indeed a tumor on my right kidney, but it was only around 1.3 centimeters. If the size of the tumor grew larger than 6 centimeters, then he would have to go in and take it out.

All of this has happened, going from surgeon to surgeon, with tumors on my kidney, and very high blood pressure. I think that I have been to every surgeon in St. Louis, all within the year 2017 and the beginning of 2018.

I am trying my best not to complain, but I am exhausted and weary. I am anxious to see what God has in store for me.

Adding to these struggles, I have been singing since I was two years of age and God has used my voice to bless others. Since I have had forty-six surgeries, I can no longer hold a note. I also have had a couple of choking spells when I was choking while eating. I need to see yet another surgeon to see if this is reversible, or is a build up of scar tissue.

CHAPTER 40

WAITING IN EXPECTATION

In the fall of 2018, I had my first consultation to discuss getting my prosthetic leg. After two hours of reviewing my case, I was told they would have to get a team together. It was going to be quite a journey.

My expectation keeps me excited. I can't wait to get behind the wheel of my car and drive again. As I said before, I've always been a motor head, a hot rod, and I have a very fast car sitting in my garage, just waiting for me to get behind the wheel and drive it. I can't wait to feel the horsepower under my right foot.

My prayer to God is to wake up with all new joints, a new leg, a new shoulder, and a new elbow. I don't want just to walk, but to run, to lay my hands on the sick, especially those people that are amputees.

I keep seeing visions of arms and legs, eyes and ears, being newly created by the hand of God right before my very eyes. I know that God would not show me these things if they were just wishful thinking. The visions are so vivid and clear, and I have had the same visions and dreams over and over. If these visions and dreams were not true, I know that God would not show them to me. I cannot wait for that day. I cannot wait until the day when I am completely restored, and renewed for the kingdom and His glory. I give Him all the praise and all the honor.

I know that God does not do anything halfway. I know that He does not break His promises, and I know that He cannot lie. For this reason, I sit and wait, and I put my trust in God alone. I have prayed every prayer that I know how to pray. I have been prayed for by so many people. Not until I get to heaven will I ever know how many people have called out my name, and held me up in prayer over these past 56 years, including relatives on both sides of my family, friends, neighbors, hundreds of prayer groups, and people I have never even met.

There have been times when I have grown weary like Moses. There have been times when I felt like I was holding onto a rope. God is holding onto one end, and I am holding onto the other...holding on for dear life. I feel, at this point in my life, that I just want to let go. I want to give it all to God, lay it at His feet, and say, "You take it, Jesus, I have done all that I can do." We should all be "letting go," and let Him have complete control.

I will not give up. I am just handing my life and my health over to the Master. It is in His hands. He is the One who already paid the price for my healing over 2000 years ago. He is the Master Carpenter, Teacher, Healer...He paid the price on Calvary with His own blood. He is the only one who can heal and restore my body. I am anxiously awaiting the day that my body is made completely whole, and that I am in in His perfect will.

CHAPTER 41

MY NEXT CHAPTER

I am finally in the process of physical rehabilitation. The therapists now come to my house twice a week to build up strength in my lower body, which has atrophied due to the six and a half years that I have been immobile. My enthusiasm and determination are pushing me to work hard to regain the strength that has been lost. I was recently measured for my prosthetic leg. To my great surprise, I received it much earlier than I thought I would. They are working with me now to get it to fit exactly. I covet your prayers, that God would give me the strength required to go through this process. It will entail being driven to a facility, and endure up to five or six hours a day in physical therapy. My body is weak, but His strength is perfect.

Jesus tells us in His Word to come to Him as little children, with childlike faith. A few years ago, my little great niece, Keely, came into my room and snuggled up to me, not understanding why I was always in bed, and not able to get out and be with the rest of the family.

A while later, Mom had gone downstairs to fix

some food for Jackson, Keely's brother. When she came back up the stairs, she looked into her bedroom, and found Keely, kneeling with her hands folded, calling out my name in prayer. She was intent on her prayer, and was not distracted at all by my mom watching her. It was such a dear, precious moment that Mom had to capture it by taking a picture. We have gazed upon that picture, and have drawn strength from the memory of her sweet prayer so many times.

In later years, each of my great nieces and nephews would tell me that they were praying for me, and that they wanted Jesus to heal me.

I, too, pray with child-like faith, and have turned my life over to Jesus. I am asking Him for a complete, divine miracle, so that I may fulfill His divine purpose and plan for my life.

This is the reason for the title of my book "Crushed and Bleeding, but the Anchor Still Holds." There is a song called "The Anchor Holds," and it has been my theme song. I cannot tell you the many times over the years that I have sung this song and clung to the words as a lifeline. Ever since I have been born, my body has been crushed, broken, and bleeding, waiting for the next catastrophe to happen and for the next hemorrhage to occur. Even in this nightmare, I remember that Jesus was broken and bleeding, and yet shed His blood that I may be healed.

I pray, as you read this book, that it will be a blessing to you and to many others. God has, time and time again, performed miracles on my behalf. Had it not been for these miracles, I would not be alive to share my story with you. My story is not over. I know what God has shown me, and I know there is coming a day that my body will be totally healed and restored. I anxiously await that day when I am able to share the story of my total healing and the restoration of my body with the world. What a glorious day that will be!

The Author

I have felt inspired for many years to write a book about my life story. I was born with hemophilia. There is no cure for this disease, and in the year 1962, when I was born, there was also no treatment for the disease. This book chronicles the many times that God has touched me, and performed miracles on my behalf. It shares the story of how He reached down His hand at the midnight hour and spared my life.

I have never known a day without pain in my 56 years of life. My body has undergone 46 surgeries, and I lost my leg in 2016 due to this terrible disease. My spirit was broken upon hearing that they would have to take my leg, but God stepped in once again to rescue me.

I have been bedridden for seven years. It is certainly not how I would have chosen to live my life, but, through it all, I have gotten so very close to God. For everything, there is a season! I believe in the scripture, in Jeremiah 29:11, that says, "For I know the plans I have for you," declares the Lord, "plans to prosper you and not to harm you, plans to give you hope and a future." When my health allowed me to attend church, one of the songs that I would sing was entitled "The Anchor Holds." For much of my life, it has felt as if I was out on the ocean, drowning, without a lifeboat to save me, but yet the anchor, which is God, my Savior, still holds.

It is my prayer that this book will touch every person that reads its pages, and that it will give hope to someone who may have a disability or a life-threatening disease. I pray that this book will encourage someone who may have experienced such a profound disappointment in your life that it has overtaken you, and you feel that you are that person out on the ocean drowning. Hold on to God! He will meet you in your hour of need, and show you great and marvelous things. May God give you miracles and blessings, as only He can give.

As I write this, I am in the process of getting my prosthetic leg. I am excited for this new chapter in my life, to once again be able to be mobile, after being bedridden for so many years. I am anxious to see where God will lead me, and how He will direct each step of my life. My trust is in Him. I have much work to do, because His return is near!

God bless you!

Darren Shelton

CPSIA information can be obtained
at www.ICGtesting.com
Printed in the USA
LVHW052227280219
609144LV00034B/1061/P